GW01376669

Guide
to
Reflexology
and
Complementary Therapies

GUIDE TO REFLEXOLOGY AND COMPLEMENTARY THERAPIES

Joyce Miller

CAXTON REFERENCE

© 2000 Caxton Editions

This edition published 2000 by Caxton Editions,
20 Bloomsbury Street, London, WC1B 3QA.

Caxton Editions is an imprint of the Caxton Publishing Group.

All rights reserved.
No part of this publication may be reproduced, stored in a retrieval system, or transmitted, in any form or by any means, electronic, mechanical, photocopying, recording or otherwise, without the prior permission of the copyright holder.

Printed and bound in India.

CONTENTS

Introduction	7
Acupuncture	15
Alexander Technique	21
Aromatherapy	27
Ayurvedic or Indian Medicine	49
Bach Flower Remedies	59
Breathing Techniques	65
Chakra Balancing	67
Chinese Medicine	73
Chiropractic	83
Chua Ka	89
Colour Therapy	91
Crystal Therapy	95
Do-in	101
Healing Touch	107
– Reflexology	111
– Acupressure	127
– Shiatsu	133

– Qigong	141
Herbalism	147
Homeopathy	155
Light Therapy	175
Magnetic Therapy	181
Meditation	187
Naturopathy	193
Osteopathy	205
T'ai Chi	211
Thermal and Cryo Therapies	215
Yoga	219
Other Healing Therapies	227

INTRODUCTION

The range of complementary or alternative medicines is large and diverse, ranging from acupuncture and aromatherapy to osteopathy and yoga. Some other less well known ones include Light therapy, Crystal therapy, Magnetic therapy and Chakra balancing. They have often been regarded as non-scientific whereas western or allopathic medicine has been considered as scientific. Most of these systems of health care are not taught in western orthodox medical training schools or universities therefore they have been regarded as non-establishment or inferior. However, attitudes have changed and rather than these systems being seen as non-scientific it is now acknowledged that they are based on different, but no less valuable, systems of theory and understanding about disease causation and treatments. Certainly allopathic medicine has developed life-saving technology and drugs but many diseases like cancer and heart disease are still major killers. People have also discovered that many of the drugs have serious side effects which may cause other health problems. The cost of medicine also makes it unavailable to many sections of the world's population.

Science has stressed that empiricism – the making and testing of models by what has been observed – as invalid but the system of biomedical science used today is not always able to explain or account for certain phenomena or effects. Alternative or complementary health systems, many of which have a longer history than modern allopathic medicine, always tried to describe, understand and work within its own acceptable reality. They stressed the importance of wellbeing and that the prevention of disease is better than treating symptoms. The emphasis of early systems of health care was holistic: the mind and body were not separate and therefore could not be treated separately. Allopathic medicine treated the symptoms of diseases not the person. Western medicine certainly prefers prevention but, since it uses chemical medication to treat symptoms, patients have come to expect to be treated by pharmaceutical means rather than addressing aspects of their own lifestyle. Complementary therapies focus on the individual and their strengths, weaknesses and circumstances. The patient is an important and active participant in their own health and treatment. Although many of the therapies do use external agents like herbs, needles, manipulation and movements to relieve symptoms, the state of wellbeing or reestablishment of health also results from balancing the relationship between the internal and external as well as establishing internal equilibrium. Complementary therapies stress self-healing, the stimulation of body energy, the importance of diet and nutrition, the use of plants and the influence of the individual themselves.

There has been a gradual shift in awareness and acceptability in the west and many more of these therapies are available. Indeed some are now recommended by orthodox medical practitioners and some basic knowledge of them is included in nursing and other medical training. Many people are now turning to other systems of health care and taking responsibility for their own health and wellbeing. With increased understanding of these other systems, such as ayurvedic medicine or Chinese medicine, it can be seen that these treatments are gentle, safe and have few side effects. In the future complementary and orthodox medicine may be increasingly integrated.

Some of the complementary therapies included in this book, such as osteopathy, acupuncture and Chinese medicine, require consultation, diagnosis and treatment by trained practitioners. This is because they have complex diagnosis and treatment procedures which cannot be self-administered. On the other hand some others, such as Bach Flower remedies or Colour therapy, can be tried and tested on a self-treatment basis as they are so safe and gentle. Those included here are a selection of the most common therapies but there are others which are also available such as Dream therapy, Biofeedback, Visualisation and Colon therapy. This selection is offered as a brief introduction to the history and origins, the theory and principles and the application and practice of the various forms of treatment. Descriptions of specific treatments are only included as example rather than full lists and if further information is desired then a specialised book dedicated to the individual therapy may be required. Similarly advice from a qualified practitioner or from specialised retail outlets such as herbalists should be sought.

Introduction

The entries are listed alphabetically, although the therapies of reflexology, acupressure, Shiatsu and Qigong are all included under the category of Healing Touch therapies.

A–Z OF COMPLEMENTARY THERAPIES

ACUPUNCTURE

History and origins

Acupuncture is an ancient Chinese therapy which involves the insertion of needles into particular key points on the body. Although acupuncture and moxibustion – the burning of the dried and powdered leaves of artemesia vulgaris on or near the skin – are separate they are very closely linked. Both techniques are used to relieve blockages in the internal energy channels. The ultimate objective of acupuncture is the regulate qi. There are many problems which can be treated with acupuncture but it is most useful for conditions such as respiratory conditions like bronchitis and asthma; eye disorders like conjunctivitis, retinitis, uncomplicated cataract and myopia in children; digestive conditions like ulcers, colitis, dysentery, constipation and diarrhoea; neurological and musculoskeletal problems like rheumatism, back pain, arthritis, migraine, neuralgia, facial palsy, Meniere's disease, painful joints and bladder problems. It can also help stress, insomnia and allergies. For addictive problems, such as smoking, acupuncture can relieve some of the withdrawal symptoms.

Acupuncture can be administered only by a trained practitioner and therefore it cannot be carried out on a self-treatment basis.

Theory and principles

Qi and blood flow through the body, its organs and the channel pathways called meridians. When it flows clearly and smoothly the body is healthy. When it is blocked illness and pain result. Blockages can be caused by an evil environmental influence such as wind, cold, fire, damp, summer heat and dryness; the patient's mental state or any physical trauma. Pain is linked to an injury or interruption in the flow of qi and acupuncture can remove any obstruction. At the same time the yin and yang forces can be out of balance. The yin and yang are complementary but opposing forces such as male/female, black/white, good/bad or hot/cold. The yin represents female, calm, dark, cold and wet. The yang is male and represents heat, light, dry and aggression. Acupuncture attempts to reestablish the balance between these two.

The points where the needles are inserted are located on meridians. These are the pathways or channels where qi flows. There were 365 points traditionally, but this number has increased and there can be as many as 2,000 now. There are 14 meridians 12 of which represent major internal organs. The control of temperature and the 'triple heater' do not relate to any specific organ but are included in the meridians. Another two, the 'governor' and the 'conception' run along the middle of the body. The governor extends from the head down to the mouth and the conception starts at the chin and runs to the base of the trunk.

Application and practice

During a consultation the acupuncturist will examine the patient using a set of formal rules in order to identify the relevant acupuncture points. The patient's skin colouring and texture, their posture and movement, their voice and tongue are examined and assessed. Questions are also asked about diet, sleep, exercise, problems, stresses and fears. The pulse is recorded on six places on the wrist which relate to main organs. These are felt and they acupuncturist can determine information about the flow of qi.

Once the sites or site of insertion has been identified the needles are inserted quickly into the skin and adjusted to the appropriate depth. The angle and depth of insertion, the methods of manipulation and the length of retention are different for different conditions and treatments. The needles are usually inserted between just below the skin up to about half an inch or 12 millimetres deep. As many as 15 needles may be used at one time but usually five or six is enough. They may be left inserted from as little as a few minutes to to half an hour. Some may be retained for several days.

The aim is to obtain qi at the site and the acupuncturist requires an indication that qi has been stimulated. This can be confirmed either by the practitioner or by the patient from the sensations experienced as the needles are manipulated. The acupuncturist can feel a grasping sensation through the needle and the patient can sense its stimulation with sensations of itching, numbness, soreness or swelling. The patient may also experience localised temperature change or a feeling of electrical energy. The different acupuncture points react in different ways but the reaction and sensations experienced are important diagnostic indicators for the practitioner.

Once the point has been located, needled and qi stimulated the acupuncturist can manipulate the needle. They may leave the needle alone or manipulate it with slow or fast insertion or changing the direction of the needle.

There are many texts which describe the location of specific points which can be used to treat specific conditions but the acupuncturist can also use other theoretical knowledge to help identify appropriate points. For example, another important aspect of the patient's condition is the status of the five phases. The five phases are earth, metal, water, wood and fire and are used to describe the relationships between certain phenomena which are organised in five phases. For example, for the organs of the bowel the gallbladder relates to the wood phase, the small intestine to the fire phase, the stomach to earth, the large intestine to metal and urinary bladder to water. For emotional conditions wood relates to anger, joy to fire, thought to earth, sorrow to metal and fear to water.

Most patients feel some improvement after four or five sessions as the effects occur quite gradually, particularly if the symptoms have been chronic. Some very long-standing conditions, such as asthma, may take longer before any change is noticed. Sometimes after the first session the symptoms may feel worse due to the effect of the energy stimulation. If no changes are felt after six or eight sessions then it is doubtful whether acupuncture can be of help.

Trials have shown that endorphins and encephalins – the body's natural pain killers – are released or stimulated by acupuncture. Acupuncture can therefore be useful to relieve pain and in China it is used as a form of anaesthesia, particularly during childbirth, dentistry and other operations.

ALEXANDER TECHNIQUE

This practice is based on the importance of correct posture in order that the body functions naturally and to its maximum potential with the minimum amount of muscular effort.

It is useful for sports exercising, breathing, arthritis, high blood pressure, back and neck pain, posture problems as well as stress, tension, anxiety, depression, insomnia, mental fatigue and poor self-image.

Although there are no specific contraindications those suffering from long term medical problems should check with their medical practitioner before starting a new regime.

History and origins
The technique was developed by Frederick Matthias Alexander who was born in 1869 on Tasmania, just off the coast of Australia. Alexander, after several early jobs, eventually became an actor and recitalist. However, he

developed a problem with his voice which he would lose during his performances. Although the condition improved after resting he could get no long term advice from doctors. Alexander spent the next ten years studying his movements and how he used his body during his performances. He observed himself in a mirror doing his recitations in order to record his actions. He eventually noticed a pattern in his movement where he drew his head back and down before he started to speak. This created tension in his back, neck and head. Alexander attempted to correct the problem by freeing his head movement so that it went up and forward and the loss-of-speech problem disappeared. Although he returned to the stage Alexander became more interested in the implications of his discovery: that the conscious mind could change subconscious muscle movements. He felt that the proper use of the mind and body could affect physical, mental and emotional well-being of many people with different problems.

Alexander continued to develop and refine his technique, and abandoned the stage in order to teach his methods. He travelled to London in 1904 where his approach was popular with other actors. He later went to America and achieved international recognition for his technique. He suffered a stroke when aged 78 but managed to recover using his own method. Alexander died in 1955 and during his career his methods were taken up by many important celebrities including George Bernard Shaw, Aldous Huxley and Lillie Langtrey.

Many athletes and dancers claim the technique helps their performance but the method can help many others who are neither athletes nor public performers. It does not treat specific conditions but aids general stress and muscular ache although tension, anxiety, asthma, headaches can be improved as well.

Application and practice

The first stage is to assess posture. Correct posture and balance are important for effective muscular effort. The head should be balanced above the spine with the shoulders relaxed. Although posture is important it is not static and correct movement is also necessary. The technique therefore stresses thinking about movement before using the muscles and body in order to use them efficiently. Movements are always proceeded by a time of self-inspection either sitting or standing.

Instruction by an Alexander teacher should start off with gentle manipulation. Some use light pushing and others pull gently. Any manipulation which is used should ease the body into a relaxed and comfortable position. The movements should be felt physically but there should be a conscious awareness as well.

Sessions may take about half an hour each and up to twenty or thirty lessons may be necessary. After the course of lessons pupils should have gained enough knowledge and understanding of the technique to continue doing it themselves. With improved posture the body will be carried in an upright position.

The technique can be practised in two positions every day, sitting at a desk and sitting on a chair. Sitting in the correct manner the head should be balanced comfortably with no tension at the shoulders. The shoulders and head should not be slumped forward as this restricts the stomach, which can affect breathing. Equally holding the body in an upright tense position is equally incorrect. With eyes open the head should be turned slowly from side to side. Then the head should be tilted upwards to look at the ceiling then down to look at the floor. The next stage involves further tilting and stretching of the head, followed by moving the whole torso up from the hips. During the movement the body should always follow the head. During the movements it is important to notice how the body reacts. There may be episodes of tightening although there should be no forcing of the body.

AROMATHERAPY

Aromatherapy is the use of essential plant oils to promote well-being and healing. The term was first used in 1928 by René-Maurice Gattefossé, a French chemist. Aroma, as a chemical term refers to organic compounds and therapy to treatment to relieve symptoms. The aroma or smell of the essential oils are an important aspect of their healing properties. Essential oils are extracted from different parts of plants which are distilled to produce the essences. They are applied to the body by massage, inhaled, used as an external application or taken as suppositories or pessaries. The part of the brain which responds to smell is found in the same area which controls emotional expression, and it is therefore not surprising that aromatherapy has many emotional and psychological benefits.

However the therapeutic benefits of aromatherapy have been disputed by orthodox medicine as there has been relatively little research done, or trials carried out, to support claims about the healing properties of essential oils.

Aromatherapy was first brought to the UK by Marguerite Maury who promoted the use of aromatherapy through massage. The use of aromatherapy has increased and is used by cosmetic and beauty therapists as well as other health professionals. It is now one of the fastest growing complementary therapies and has now been accepted as an acceptable treatment in both psychological and physical conditions.

History and origins

Gattefossé first noted the benefit of essential oils when he burnt his hand in a laboratory experiment. He applied lavender oil which was nearby and his hand healed quickly and without the expected scarring. He then went on to examine and analyse individual oils and categorise them according to properties such as antiseptic, detoxifying, stimulating and calming.

The use of essential oils was recorded in Arabic medicine and Avicenna was thought to have discovered the process of distilling plants in the 10th century. However other evidence suggests that the process of distilling was also used in early Indian medicine.

Aromatherapy

In Egypt fragrant essential oils were used in beauty products but were also thought to increase spiritual well-being. Frankincense, myrrh, and juniper were used for their medicinal properties. The Greeks also believed in the benefits of scented massages and baths. By the eighteenth century aromatic oils were used in perfumes and to help treat illness, as well as disguise unpleasant bodily smells from lack of personal hygiene. Aromatic pomanders were also believed to protect against diseases such as the plague. Native North Americans used aromatic herbs mixed with tobacco smoke as a form of cure.

By the nineteenth and twentieth centuries the therapeutic uses of essential oils were increasingly ignored as the cosmetic and perfume side developed. The attractiveness of cosmetic perfumes was in part due to their pleasant aromas, but also because they were suggestive of certain personal qualities or taste. Feeling good or attractive because of the presence of essential oils was not recognised as being part of the reason people like perfumes.

Margaret Maury worked on the use of essential oils in the 1950s, Her work was based on observations made during World War II when soldiers were treated with oils instead of penicillin. She observed essential oils had therapeutic uses as a massage and allopathic treatment.

Currently most people receive aromatherapy treatments in the form of massage. Most aromatherapists are trained massage therapists but many nursing courses are starting to include aromatherapy massage training as well. Massage is used by many health practitioners including osteopaths and physiotherapists and nurses have now recognised that it can play an important role in the management of pain and stress.

Theory and principles - Essential Oils

Volatile oils are fragrant constituents of plants and obtained by distillation or cold compress. Synthetic oils, even when they are chemically very similar, lack the true elements which make the oils therapeutically useful. The oils can be obtained from the leaves, flowers, fruits, grasses, wood, bark, bulbs, resin or roots. The amount of oil produced from one plant varies with the species. Rose petals produce only a very small amount whereas lavender, lemon or garlic produce far greater amounts. The oils are stored in amber coloured bottles to protect them from light.

The oils are a mixture of organic compounds

including esters, ketones, alcohols, acids and ethers. These organic compounds have quite distinct therapeutic actions. For example esters have an antispasmodic and calming effect, alcohols and phenols are antibacterial and oxides have an expectorant effect. The oils can be used in a wide range of physical, mental and emotional conditions.

As with herbal medicine the climate and growing conditions can influence the qualities of the essential oil produced. The difference may mean that some oils may be contraindicated because of potential side effects. In particular some oils are recommended to be avoided by pregnant women, babies and young children. Basil, citronella, clary sage, clove, fennel, hysop, juniper, marjoram, myrrh, cedarwood atlas, peppermints, rosemary and thyme should not be used during pregnancy. Skin reactions, allergic reactions, abortive and neurological side effects have been recorded. Basil, cardamom, ginger, lemon, fennel, lemongrass, melissa, pine, rosemary, cajuput, black pepper, tea tree and thyme may irritate the skin. Cinnamon should not be used on the skin at all. Lemon, lemongrass, mandarin and orange oil increase the sensitivity of the skin to sun. Camphor, fennel, hyssop and rosemary should not be used by anyone with epilepsy and hyssop, rosemary and thyme should be avoided by those suffering from high blood pressure.

There has been a lack of control over the production, labelling and selling of essential oils which has contributed to poor levels of understanding about potential side effects. The medical profession has voiced concern that the general public have developed an impression that they are quite harmless because they are natural products. At the moment there is no legislation which guarantees the quality of oils, whether they are safe or have been adulterated with the addition of other oil to reduce the price. There is an Aromatherapy Trades Council which analyse and test oils to ensure they are pure and produced to the highest standard.

Research
The oils found in thyme, sage and tarragon have an antibacterial effect. Peppermint has a calmative effect on smooth intestinal muscle. Sandalwood, chamomile, marjoram and lavender have a sedative effect and clove, basil, neroli and ylang ylang have stimulant effects.

Aromatherapy

Application and practice
The administration of essential oils can be internal by the mouth, rectum or vaginal or by external absorption through the skin by massage. Essential oils are very concentrated and it is important that they are used carefully. As the essential oils should not be massaged undiluted onto the skin the use of a vegetable-based carrier oil is important. Usually about six drops in two teaspoons of oil is the recommended dilution. Tests have shown that massage using lavender oil resulted in lavender oil components present in the blood stream after five minutes. They reached maximum levels after twenty minutes and returned to pre-massage state within ninety minutes. Aromas can also be inhaled via vapours. A few drops of essential oil can be used in baths as the heat of the water aids absorption through the skin and by inhalation through the steam at the same time. Inhalation or vaporisation are used for respiratory conditions, sleeping problems and relaxation and can be administered by heating the oil directly or via steam when mixed with water. However, too high a concentration of oils or overexposure may cause headaches and skin and eye irritation.

    Studies have shown that benefits are obtained

from both the massage element as well as the essential oils themselves. Reduced anxiety, relaxation and improved mood have been reported, although no difference in heart or respiratory rates or blood pressure have been observed.

Aromatherapy is now offered in conjunction with orthodox medical practice. It is especially useful in cancer care, intensive care, HIV and AIDS units, children's wards, midwifery and neonatal care, burns units and with those who have learning difficulties. The benefits gained from aromatherapy treatment include relaxation, reduction in stress and anxiety, reduction in pain, wound healing – particularly burns – and improvement in infections, constipation, improved self-esteem and increased immune status.

The oils and their use

Basil *(Ocimum basilicum)* – grown in Egypt. It has a sweet, spicy fragrance and is soothing and uplifting. It aids concentration and is good for toning tired and aching muscles. Basil mixes well with lavender, geranium and bergamot. It can irritate the skin and should not be used during pregnancy.

Aromatherapy

Benzoin *(Styrax benzoin)* – grown in Thailand. Benzoin has a sweet, warm aroma and soothes and stimulates when used as an inhalation. It is also useful for aching muscles when used as a massage oil.

Begamot *(Citrus bergamia)* – grown in Sicily. It has a strong, fresh citrus fragrance and has a stimulating effect. It can be used in skin care and mixes well with other oils.

Black Pepper *(Pier nigrum)* – grown in Indonesia. Black Pepper was used in India 4000 years ago. It has a pungent aroma and has a warm, stimulating effect. It is useful in a massage for dancers and athletes as it helps prevent muscle stiffness. It can also be blended with lavender, marjoram and rosemary. Only very small amounts should be used, no more than three or four drops. It can also irritate some skin types.

Cajeput *(Melaleauca minor)* – grown in Vietnam. Cajeput is a warming oil. It can be used in inhalations to clear the sinuses and can also help spots and oily skin. It has an irritant effect so must be used with caution.

Camphor *(white)* *(Cinnamomum camphora)* – grown in China. This oil is native to Japan and China and the oil is useful for oily or spotty skin. It can also be used as an insect repellent. It should be used sparingly and avoided by those suffering from epilepsy.

Cardamom *(Elettaria cardamomum)* – grown in Guatemala. This is a sweet and spicy oil which was used by Egyptians in perfumes and incense. It is also used in Indian cooking. It aids digestion and, when used as a bath oil, has a refreshing and invigorating effect. It can irritate the skin.

Cedarwood Atlas *(Cedrus atlantica)* – grown in Morroco. Cedarwood oil is useful for oily or spotty skin as it is a mild astringent. It has a warm, woody aroma and is a pleasant room fragrance. It is used as an incense in Tibetan temples. It should not be used during pregnancy.

Chamomile *(Roman)* *(Anthemis nobilis)* – grown in England. Chamomile is a gentle, soothing oil. It has a light fragrance and is good for skin care and for those with fair hair. It mixes well with lavender.

Cinnamon leaf *(Cinnamomum zeylanicum)* – grown in Sri Lanka. Cinnamon is a warm, spicy oil which is especially pleasant as a room fragrance. It blends well with orange and clove and has antiseptic properties. It is a skin irritant and should be used carefully.

Citronella *(Cymbopogon nardus)* – grown in Sri Lanka. It has a strong lemon aroma and is useful as an insect repellent. It is also used for tired aching feet.

Clary Sage *(Salvia sclarea)* – grown in France. Clary sage has a nutty aroma and has strong stimulating effect. It should not be used with alcohol. However it can be used as a relaxant and is useful for dandruff and for oily skin and hair. Not to be used during pregnancy.

Clove *(Eugenia carophyllata)* – grown in Madacasgar. Clove is used to relieve toothache and it also has antiseptic properties. It can be used as a mosquito repellent. It should not be used during pregnancy and can irritate the skin.

Coriander *(Coriandrum savitum)* – grown in Russia. A sweet-smelling spice coriander is a good massage oil and helps tired, stiff and aching muscles. It is a refreshing addition to bath water.

Cypress *(Cupressus sempervirens)* – grown in France. Cypress is a smoky, woody oil and has relaxing and refreshing properties. It has an astringent effect when used on the skin, particularly when used as foot bath, and it can also act as an insect repellent. It mixes well with lavender and sandalwood.

Eucalyptus *(Eucalyptus globulus)* – grown in China. Best known for its vaporising and antiseptic properties eucalyptus is especially useful in winter. It is a pleasant massage oil for tired muscles. It also mixes well with lavender and pine.

Fennel *(Foeniculum vulgare)* – grown in Hungary. Fennel is particularly useful for skin care It has a sweet, aniseed aroma but should not be used with young children, epileptics and during pregnancy.

Frankincense *(Bowelllia thurifera)* – grown in Somalia. It has been used in incense in churches and temples for centuries. Frankincense slows breathing and helps control tension and concentration. It is also useful for skin care, especially dry or mature skin.

Geranium *(Pelargonium graveolens)* – grown in Egypt. A pale, green oil geranium has a sweet, floral aroma. It can be used on all skin types and has refreshing and balancing emotional effect. It mixes well with lavender and bergamot.

Ginger *(Zingiber officinale)* – grown in China. Ginger has warming properties and is useful in treating aches and pains. It can be used as a massage oil or added to the bath. It blends well with orange and other citrus-based oils. It can irritate the skin.

Grapefruit *(Citrus x paradisi)* – grown in Israel. Extracted by cold compression grapefruit oil has refreshing and uplifting properties. It has a sharp fragrance and is especially useful in nervous conditions as well as improving oily skin.

Hyssop *(Hyssopus officinalis)* – grown in France. The aroma has antiseptic properties and is used to vaporise and clear rooms. Should not be used during pregnancy or if suffering from high blood pressure or epilepsy.

Jasmine *(Jasminum officinale)* – grown in Morocco. Jasmine oil can only be obtained from flowers picked at night when their fragrance is at its best. It is an expensive oil but only needs to be used in very small quantities. It has an beautiful floral fragrance and is especially useful in skin care, for dry and sensitive skins. It is also relaxing when used in a massage oil. It also is reputed to have aphrodisiac properties.

Juniper *(Juniperus communis)* – grown in Austria. Distilled from berries the oil has astringent and antiseptic properties. It is beneficial for oily skins and, when added to bath water, has a calming effect. It should not be used during pregnancy.

Lavender *(Lavendula angustifolia)* – grown in Bulgaria or France. Lavender is the most commonly used essential oil. Used in the bath it has a calming and soothing effect. When applied to the skin it has antiseptic properties. It also mixes very well with many other oils and adds a pleasant floral fragrance.

Lemon *(Citrus limonum)* – grown in Sicily. Lemon's astringent properties are especially useful for oily skin but it should not be applied directly to the skin in sunlight. Lemon oil has a strong, tangy citrus aroma. It should only be used in very small amounts – for example only three drops in a bath as it may cause skin irritation.

Lemongrass *(Cymbogon citratus)* – grown in Guatemala. Lemongrass has a stronger, sweeter lemon aroma than lemon oil. It has antiseptic properties and is useful for tired, aching feet. It is a useful stimulating massage oil and when used in a vaporiser it refreshes and deodorises. It can also be used as an insect repellent. It should not be used on the skin in direct sunlight as it may cause irritation. Only three drops of the oil should be used in the bath water.

Lime *(Citrus aurantifolia)* – grown in Mexico. Lime has a refreshing and sweet citrus aroma. It has antiseptic properties and is useful for oily skins. It also eases muscle and joint aches. It can be used in the sun and should not cause irritation.

Mandarin *(Citrus reticulata)* – grown in Italy. Mandarin has a gentle, sweet fragrance and has a calming effect. Used in a massage oil it aids digestive problems. It is safe to use in a massage oil to ease stretch marks during pregnancy. Do not apply directly to the skin in direct sunlight.

Marjoram *(Origanum marjorana)* – grown in Egypt. With a peppery fragrance marjoram has warming and relaxing properties. It can ease muscular aches and nervous tension. It can be mixed with lavender and a few drops are pleasant in a bath. Only small amounts should be used as its sedative action can be powerful. Do not used during pregnancy.

Melissa true *(Melissa officinalis)* – grown in Egypt. Melissa is also known as lemon balm. It has calming and relaxing properties. Only three drops should be used in the bath and it may cause skin irritation.

Myrrh *(Commiphora myrrha)* – grown in Somalia. Myrrh oil is extracted from tree resin. It has a hot, smoky aroma and is useful for dry, cracked skin. It can also be used as a mouth rinse. Should not be used during pregnancy.

Neroli *(orange blossom) (Citrus aurantium)* – grown in Sicily. Neroli oil is distilled from the Seville orange tree. It has a pleasant floral aroma and can be used on mature and sensitive skins as well as scar tissue. It can reduce stress and anxiety. It is an expensive oil but can be blended with jasmine and rose.

Niaouli *(Melaleuca viridiflora)* – grown in Madagascar. This is a sweet-smelling oil with antiseptic properties. It is useful for problem skin, especially cases of acne and irritated skin. It can also be applied as a chest rub.

Orange sweet *(Citrus sinensis)* – grown in USA. Orange oil has a fresh, twangy fragrance. It is refreshing and relaxing and is particularly pleasant when blended with a spicy oil like clove or cinnamon. Use no more than two drops in the bath and do not apply directly to the skin in sunlight.

Palmarosa *(Cymbopogon martinii)* – grown in Madagascar. Palmarosa has a sweet, floral aroma. It has uplifting and refreshing properties. When added to almond oil it is useful in skin care and as a moisturiser helps both mature and spotty skin.

Patchouli *(Pogostemom patchouly)* – grown in Indonesia. A strong, earthy fragrance patchouli is useful in skin care, particularly oily and spotty skin types.

Peppermint *(Mentha piperita)* – grown in USA. Peppermint is a widely-used oil in both medicines and confectionery. It is soothing and refreshing and can be used in a massage oil to aid aching muscles. It blends well with juniper and rosemary to make a stimulating bath and it is also pleasant when used as a foot soak. Use no more than three drops in a bath as it may irritate sensitive skins.

Petitgrain *(Citrus aurantium)* – grown in Paraguay. Distilled from orange blossom leaves petitgrain has a fresh, flowery aroma. Added to a bath it has a refreshing effect and in a massage oil its gentle astringent properties give it a pleasant deodorant effect. It relieved stress and anxiety and blends well with other oils such as geranium, lavender and orange.

Pine *(Scots) (Pinus sylvestris)* – grown in Austria. Pine oil is pale yellow and has a strong, sharp resiny fragrance. It is refreshing and stimulating and also has antiseptic properties. It blends well with tea tree and eucalyptus and is a pleasant room freshener when used in a vaporiser. It should always be diluted and may cause skin irritation.

Rose Otto *(Rosa damascena)* – grown in Bulgaria. Because it is difficult to produce rose oil is very expensive however only a very small amount is required as it is very concentrated. It is useful for dry and mature skins, as well as promoting a feeling of wellbeing. It also has a reputation as having aphrodisiac properties.

Rosemary *(Rosemarinus officinalis)* – grown in Spain. Rosemary has an invigorating fragrance which stimulates the mind and relieves aching muscles. It is also useful for greasy hair and dandruff. Do not use when pregnant or suffer from epilepsy or high blood pressure. It may also irritate sensitive skins.

Sandalwood *(Santalum album)* – grown in India. This has a warm, woody aroma which is very relaxing. It is useful for both dry and oily skin types as it has both moisturising and astringent properties. It has also been used as an aphrodisiac.

Tea Tree *(Melaleuca alternifolia)* – grown in

Australia. Tea tree has a strong antiseptic fragrance. It is a stimulating, cleansing oil which has many applications. Tree tree can be used in massage oils, vaporisers and in baths. It may cause some skin irritation.

Thyme *(Thymus vulgaris)* – grown in Spain. Thyme has both medicinal and culinary uses. It has a strong fragrance and has antiseptic properties. Thyme should not be used when pregnant or suffering from high blood pressure and it may irritate sensitive skins.

Vetiver *(vetiveria zizanoides)* – grown in Java. With a woody, earthy fragrance vetiver has a gentle relaxing effect. It is very useful in massage oil or added to bath water and can also be blended with other oils.

Violet *(Viola odorata)*
This gentle oil promotes wellbeing and confidence.

Ylang Ylang *(Cananga odorata)* – grown in Madagascar. This is an exotic, sweet and floral soothing and sensual oil. It is useful for both dry and oily skin, and helps relieve stress when used

Aromatherapy

in massage oil. It also mixes well with other citrus and floral oils.

The best massage oil bases are avocado, grapeseed, soya bean, almond, peach kernel, wheatgerm and jojoba.

AYURVEDIC OR INDIAN MEDICINE

Ayurveda is based on ancient Indian philosophy and theory about prevention of disease and health care in general.

It can be used for all usual diseases and conditions which western medicine treats. For those suffering from agitation, sleep problems, depression and general anxiety or nervous states ayurvedic medicine is useful as it promotes a general feeling of wellbeing.

The fundamental philosophy stresses moderation and balance in all aspects of life.

History and origins

The name ayurveda comes from two Sanskrit words – ayus meaning life and veda meaning science. Literally ayurveda means science of life. It dates as far back as 5,000 years although it is probably older. It originated in the Atharvaveda and the Rigveda, ancient Hindu scriptures. Later the first Sanskrit medical treatises, the Carak and the Sushruta Samhitas were produced. The theories of ayurveda have developed from the experience and wisdom of generations and it is not only a system of healing and prevention but a form of lifestyle.

Theory and principles

There are five elements – earth, water, fire, air and ether (or space). These are represented in the human body as three humours or forces – the tridosha. The tridosha controls the mind, body and spirit or consciousness. The vata dosha represents air and ether and is responsible for bodily and nervous function. When it is disturbed it manifests itself with gas or nervous energy and pain. The pitta dosha represents fire and water, and governs enzymes and hormones. It is responsible for digestion, temperature, hunger, thirst and mental activity. When the pitta dosha is out of balance it causes acid and bile production leading to inflammation. The kapha dosha is composed of earth and water, and controls general stability. It regulates the other two doshas and maintains the body's tissues, strength and patience. When it is disordered its manifests itself in the production of mucous which leads to swelling. The main qualities of vata are dry, cold,

Ayurvedic or Indian medicine

light, irregularity, mobility, and roughness. Pitta is associated with hot, light, fluid, putrid, pungent and sour. Kapha is heavy, unctuous, cold, dense, soft and smooth. One, or sometimes two, of the dosha is dominant in each person but ideally the three should be in harmony and balanced.

There are also seven tissues or dhatus and three waste products or malas. The dhatus sustain the body. The first, rasa or sap, comes from digested food and includes tissue fluids and plasma. The second, blood, invigorates the body and includes red blood cells. Flesh stabilises the body and includes muscles tissue. Fat functions as a lubricant and includes adipose tissue. Bone is a supportive tissue and marrow helps bone. The final dhatu, shukra, includes the sex fluids and controls reproduction. The malas are the waste products of food and drink. There are three principal categories – urine, faeces and sweat. There is a fourth type which includes fatty excretion from the skin, ear wax, saliva, hairs and nails. According to ayurvedic theory the bowels should be evacuated once a day and urine passed six times a day.

In order to achieve balance the constitution of an individual has to be identified. There are seven possibilities: vata, pitta, kapha, vata-pitta, pitta-kapha, vata-kapha and vata-pitta-kapha. Everyone's basic constitution is determined by their genetic background and it cannot be changed however, equilibrium can still be obtained by balancing the dominant dosha with the others.

There are some simple characteristics linked with the different doshas.

Vata people are often thin and either very tall or very short. Their hair is often curly but may be thin. They enjoy sweet, sour and salty food. Vata personalities are often creative, alert, restless, talkative and walk very fast, although they tend to tire easily. They are quick to understand but have a poor memory. They also have little willpower, tolerance or confidence, and are generally anxious and nervous. They usually require little sleep and although they make money they tend to spend it rapidly and so are usually poor.

Pitta people are usually of medium height with thin reddish or brown hair. They have a good appetite and digestion and enjoy sweet, bitter food and cold drinks. They have a strong metabolism. They do not like sunlight, heat or hard work. They are intelligent and are good speakers although they have a tendency to anger, hate and jealousy. They like to be in charge. They need moderate amounts of sleep. They enjoy luxuries and tend to be quite well-off.

Kapha constitution means that people are big and often overweight. They have thick, dark and wavy hair. They have a slow digestion and enjoy bitter and astringent tastes. They move slowly but have a good stamina and are generally quite healthy and peaceful. They are quite tolerant, calm and loving although they can be possessive, envious and greedy. They have a good memory. They require long periods of sleep and tend to be wealthy as they hold onto their money.

By keeping the doshas in harmony then the body, mind and spirit will also be balanced which will keep disease away. If illness or disease is experienced then healing is possible through nature but only if the doshas are balanced. In general ayurvedic philosophy recommends a moderate lifestyle where diet (mostly vegetarian), exercise (possibly yoga), meditation and the chanting of mantras are daily routines. As required other therapies are used, such as herbal medicine and cleansing and purging.

Application and practice
Ayurvedic medicine identifies three categories of disease. Adhyatmika -type diseases originate from

inside the body. They include hereditary diseases, congenital ones and diseases caused by a combination of the doshas. Adhibhautiak illnesses originate outside the body and include injuries from accidents and illnesses caused by bacteria and viruses. Adhidaivika diseases come from supernatural sources and are caused by fate, planetary influences, curses and yearly changes.

The main cause of disease is ama which is formed when there is a decrease in enzyme activity. This can be caused by improperly digested food and it travels through the body causing blockages. Ama can mix with doshas and can affect an already weak or stressed organ or part of the body. Amaya means disease as it translates as 'coming from ama'. The main principle of treatment by ayurvedic medicine is the elimination of ama and the restoration of balance of the doshas.

A disease is named in one of six ways: from the misery it causes, its main symptom, its main physical sign, its physical nature, the doshas involved or the main organ involved. As an illness progresses the ayurvedic doctor tries to identify the site of origin, how the disease was communicated and travelled and where it manifested itself. The site of manifestation is

Ayurvedic or Indian medicine

usually different from the site of origin. This method of identification helps the doctor prescribe suitable treatments.

Removal of disease and ama also restores the individual to health, but it requires a diagnosis and treatment which considers individual mental and physical states as well as the person's social world and environment. An examination by a practitioner of ayurvedic medicine involves an examination of pulse, urine and physical features by touch, observation and questioning.

Ayurveda theory recognises two courses of treatment which are based on the condition of the patient. The first is prevention or prophylaxis for the healthy individual who wishes to maintain a healthy state. The second is therapeutic for the ill person who wants to be restored to health. Once a healthy state has been reestablished then prophylaxis is recommended to maintain wellbeing.

Therapeutic treatment is based on three principles – purification, alleviation or a combination of the two. Purification therapy or pañchakarma involves a five action treatment which may all be used or only a combination. They include emetics, purgatives, enemas, inhalations or nasal drops and finally leeches or bloodletting. Since the treatment has fairly severe physical outcomes they are administered over several days. Alleviation therapy used honey, butter or ghee and sesame or castor oil to eliminate the different doshas.

Much of ayurvedic medicine overlaps with culinary laws. Indeed many ayurvedic medicines can be found in the kitchen. Certain rules should be followed such as avoiding mixing contrary foods like butter and honey, alkalies and salts, and milk and fish. Many medicines are composed of fruit and plant extracts or from minerals. They are taken in the form of juices, powders, infusions, decoctions made from boiling plants in water, pastes and oils, pills, alcoholic fermentations or distillations of plant material and bhasmas which are ash residues from the calcination of metals, plants and animal products.

Ayurveda is a sophisticated system of medicine which has a long history. Like many other forms of alternative or complementary medicine it considers the whole person and their relation to their external world in order to diagnose, treat and reestablish equilibrium. Since it is such a complex and specialised form of treatment it cannot be self-administered therefore a trained practitioner should be consulted for advice,

Ayurvedic or Indian medicine

information and therapy.

BACH FLOWER REMEDIES

These consists of 38 flower-based formulas which can be used to treat emotional problems. Each formula contains the distilled and diluted essence of a particular flower which is then mixed with alcohol – usually brandy.

The problems which can be helped using these remedies are emotional ones such as fear, shyness, anger and resentment, low self-esteem and sadness. As the remedies contain alcohol those who avoid alcohol may not be able to use them, however the treatments usually involve much dilution which reduces the alcohol content greatly. Some allergic responses have also been observed, and those who are prescribed strong mood-changing medication such as tranquillisers, or are addicted to drugs or alcohol, may not respond well to the therapy.

History and origins
The use and importance of flowers has a long

history. Specific flowers often had important symbolic meaning such as rosemary for remembrance. Flowers were also used for medicinal, magical and religious purposes. Societies throughout the world had their own uses for different native plants some of which have now, in the twentieth century, been shown to have therapeutic effects.

In the 1930s Dr Edward Bach observed that some of his patients often manifested emotional symptoms before they developed physical illnesses. The emotional symptoms included fear, depression, worry and anxiety. He also noted that those who experienced the emotional symptoms were less able to resist or recover from the physical disease. He acknowledged that there was a close relationship between mind and body, and he became convinced that disease could be prevented or cured by treating the underlying emotional causes. He began treating patients with flower essences and noted their different reactions. He eventually developed the 38 rescue remedies which are now called the Bach Flower Remedies.

The Bach Flower Remedies do not treat specific illnesses but the physical condition is improved as the emotional symptoms are treated.

The remedies are not the same as homeopathy as the essences and dilutions are different. Homeopathy remedies are very much more dilute than the Bach Flower Remedies.

Theory and principles
The Bach Flower essences work on energy. Flowers plucked at dawn have the most energy and this is transferred to the water in which they are soaked. This liquid is then enhanced, diluted and strengthened. They are then added to brandy to preserve them.

Before use it is necessary to decide which ones are needed but although they can be mixed the number should be limited to six. Because the remedies have quite personal effect there are no certainties about how long treatment should take. Improvement may be noted after two or three weeks or it may take several months. Some changes may be noticed after a few weeks but full recovery may take longer as the effects are so subtle. However, as they are completely natural they are not toxic or addictive. Some reactions such as mild skin rash or diarrhoea may be noted. These may be part of the changes which the remedy is stimulating but if they are uncomfortable then the remedy may be stopped.

Another alternative remedy may be necessary. If there is absolutely no change then it may be necessary to reassess the situation and problem.

Application and practice

For immediate relief the remedies are either taken as a few undiluted drops of concentrate placed directly on the tongue or mixed in water or juice. For longer term use a dosage solution can be used. Two to four drops of concentrate are added to a teaspoon of brandy. This is then mixed with water in a one-ounce dropper bottle. Four to six drops of dosage should be taken four times a day. The concentrate can also be used externally by applying it directly to the temples, wrists, under arms or ears.

In order to pick the correct remedy a professional practitioner can be consulted. Advice may also be available from the retail outlet selling the remedies. There are also a number of specialist books available which contain details and information about the use of the remedies. The other alternative is to try and experiment on a self-administration basis as the remedies are quite safe.

The treatments can be used by all ages and some of the remedies and their effects are listed below.

Bach Flower Remedies

Agrimony – treats those who are internally disturbed or who may abuse substances. Helps restore cheerfulness and optimism.

Aspen – helps those who are anxious and fearful.

Cherry Plum – is useful for those who are afraid of losing control, who suffer from temper outbursts and who have self-destructive habits as it helps increase the ability to control feelings of pressure.

Clematis – can be used for those experiencing loss of attention and concentration as it increases positive feelings and interest.

Gorse – helps feelings of despair and negativity by increasing hope, belief and optimism.

Holly – reduces feelings of envy and hatred or resentment of self and of others by increasing toleration and affection.

Impatiens – addresses feelings of impatience by increasing toleration and understanding.

Mustard – is helpful for feelings of sadness and

melancholia by increasing happiness and stability.

Oak – is useful for those who are workaholics and neglect themselves or their loved ones.

Pine – helps those who experience guilt and self reproach by increasing an appropriate attitude to responsibility.

Rescue remedy – helps physical and emotional crises. As it is a mixture it is helpful in a range of different problems or crises.

Star of Bethlehem – helps shock trauma and sorrow by releasing the emotional tensions associated with events.

Vervain – is suitable for people whose fanaticism has got out of control by increasing self-control and calmness.

Wild Rose – can be used for those who are apathetic, bored, disinterested in life by increasing vitality and interest.

Willow – helps feelings of bitterness, brooding or of injustice by improving optimism.

BREATHING TECHNIQUES

Pursed lip breathing
Pursed lip breathing is a technique which helps those who are very short of breath. It helps them breathe more easily during physical exercise.

It is particularly effective for those suffering from asthma, bronchitis, emphysema and other chronic respiratory conditions. It may also be helpful to control breathing during periods of acute stress.

Application and practice
Pursed-lip breathing is quite easy. Inhale through the nose, pucker the lips and then exhale slowly through the mouth. This type of exhalation builds up pressure in the lungs and airways which helps to keep them open for longer

Diaphragmatic breathing
This form of breathing means that respiration is done from the diaphragm rather than the upper

chest. It provides a better air intake and strengthens the lungs.

It is useful for those with asthma, emphysema, bronchitis and other chronic obstructive airways ailments. It is also useful in relieving stress.

Application and practice

Breathing is usually done subconsciously and mostly the chest muscles are used. For those who have respiratory problems chest breathing is not always adequate. Breathing using the diaphragmatic muscles increases the intake of air. It is easy to learn, although it is slightly unnatural at first. When taking a deep inhalation the chest is expanded and the abdomen pulled in. The abdomen is then relaxed and distended during exhalation. In diaphragmatic breathing the abdomen is pushed out during inhalation and pulled in during exhalation. To feel if it is being done properly place your fingers under your rib cage. The fingers should lift as the abdomen rises and distends.

Diaphragmatic breathing takes a bit of practice, but pursed-lip and diaphragmatic breathing can be combined with inhalation using the diaphragm and exhalation through pursed lips.

CHAKRA BALANCING

The body has seven major energy centres known as chakras. It is important to keep these centres in harmony and chakra balancing is achieved through a combination of meditation, colour therapy and crystal therapy.

It is useful in many physical problems or diseases. Chakra balancing is also helpful for those experiencing stress, anxiety, tension and depression.

History and origins
Chakra balancing has been used in ayurvedic or Indian healing for many generations. It is also related to the principles and practices of yoga. According to ayurvedic theory people are composed of three bodies: the physical or material one, the astral or conscious body and the causal or absolute body. To some extent these correspond to the more western theory of body, mind and spirit.

Theory and principles

As we grow and mature we learn more about our astral bodies but to develop understanding about the causal body much learning and consciousness is necessary. It is believed that the three bodies are connected through seven chakras which exist in the astral and causal bodies. Chakra means wheel in Sanskrit and they are often illustrated as spinning energy wheels. The chakras supply energy to the body through channels or nadi. These nadi are very close to the Chinese system of meridians.

The chakras

The middle chakra corresponds to the spinal centre of the physical body. The lowest chakra is located at the bottom of the spine and the highest at the level of the head. Each chakra controls the function of a particular biological system, although they also have mental, spiritual and emotional characteristics.

Muladhara, is the first chakra, swadhistana the second. The swadhistana controls the sexual and elimination functions. The third chakra is the manipura and it relates to the digestive system of the physical body, and to instinct found in the unconscious body. The anahata, which controls

Chakra balancing

the heart and circulatory system, is the fourth chakra. It is also connected to selfless love and compassion. The fifth chakra is the visshuda which controls respiration as well as relating to intelligence and the ability to communicate. The sixth chakra is the ajna. It is often known as the third eye as it is located between the eye brows. It is associated with the autonomic nervous system and the pituitary gland in the physical body. In the other bodies it relates to perception, intuition, the higher brain functions and awareness of self. The last chakra is the sahasrara and is located on the cerebral cortex. It controls all the body functions of the physical body and in the other levels it controls the union of the three bodies.

Application and practice

Those who use chakra balancing believe that it releases blockages in energy flows in the body. These blockages may be caused by internal or external problems and can cause illness or disease in the part of the body which is affected as well affect the mental and emotional aspects related to that chakra. Treatment may concentrate solely on the affected chakra although some practitioners believe that the chakras must all be treated together in order to ensure harmony and balance.

Each chakra has an associated colour therefore some treatments recommend using particular colours to relieve the blockage.

Muladhara – associated with red, controls physical sensations and the genito-urinary and reproductive systems

Swadhistana – associated with orange, controls sexual desire and other emotions.

Manipura – associated with yellow, controls power, anger and dreams as well as the digestive system and adrenal glands.

Anahata – associated with green, controls love and compassion and affects the heart and circulatory system.

Visshuda – associated with blue, controls intellect and communication as well as respiration and the thyroid gland.

Ajna – associated with indigo, controls intellect, intuition and awareness of self as well as the autonomic system and pituitary gland.

Chakra balancing

Sahasrara – associated with violet, controls the imagination and self, the cerebral cortex, nervous system and pineal gland.

The use of a specific colour can influence chakras either by wearing clothes of a particular colour, creating an environment based on the same colour, wearing colour-tinted glasses or using coloured lights. Food of a particular colour is also thought by some to affect the corresponding chakra. To ensure a harmony of chakras food of all colours should be eaten. Crystals can also be used to balance the chakras by being placed on the body at the site of the affected chakra.

CHINESE MEDICINE

Chinese medicine has a long history some of which can be traced in texts, legends and practice. According to legend the origins are associated with three emperors: Fu Xi, Shen Nong and Huang Di. Huang Di is known as the originator of traditional Chinese medicine and produced a text Yellow Emperor's Inner Classic (Huang Di Nei Jing) which includes much of the form of Chinese medicine which is used today. One text covers theory of yin and yang and the effects of the seasons, and the other covers therapeutic practice in the form of acupuncture and moxibustion.

History and origins
During the Han dynasty from 206 BC to 219 AD the Chinese empire was reunited and a stable autocratic social order was created. During this dynasty there was an expansion and consolidation of the Chinese culture to incorporate Confucian doctrine and the philosophy of yin and yang.

Some of the early theories of medicine and healing included many magical and supernatural concepts. They did not refer to acupuncture, specific energy points or channels. During the first or second century AD the text Classic of Difficult Issue (Nan Jing) was compiled, This text documented a change in emphasis as there was a systematic organisation of theory and practice of acupuncture which identified body structure, illnesses, diagnosis and treatment, with no reference to magical or supernatural elements.

There were other texts produced including Treatise on Cold Damage (Shang Han Lun) and Survey of Important Elements from the Golden Cabinet and Jade Container (Jin Gui Yao Lue). The Barefoot Doctor's Manual included many folk herbal remedies and medical traditions which were practised by the majority of the non-literate peasant population of the Chinese empire. With the fall of the Han dynasty there was a period of disruption followed by the Sui, then the Tang, dynasties. During this period Daoism and Buddhism influences were seen in medical practice. After the Tang dynasty the practice of medicine during the Sung dynasty became increasingly specialised. Herbal remedies and recipes increased which reflected the yin and yang

Chinese medicine

natures of the herbs. The education of doctors also became more formalised during the Sung dynasty.

From 1368 to 1911, during the dynasties of the Ming and Qing, medical experts explored the relationship between disease causation and appropriate therapies. During the nineteenth century western influences were felt in China and, with the use of western technology and knowledge, traditional Chinese medical philosophy was threatened. The teaching of acupuncture was abandoned at the Imperial Medical College in 1822. With the fall of the Manchu rulers practitioners of traditional medicine were isolated and increasingly criticised. Western medical philosophy became established. After the 1930s it was referred to as Zhong Yi and attempted to create a disciplined and scientific philosophy. By the 1950s Chairman Mao encouraged a return to traditional methods in order to develop it as a rival system to western medical science. In 1956 four colleges of Chinese medicine were created and currently in China, Zhong Yi, is a fully accepted system of medical practice.

Theory and principles

The philosophy of Chinese medicine is underpinned by the theory of yin and yang. They represent opposing, but complementary, energies which are necessary for equilibrium. They are used to understand the processes of physiology and pathology in the human organism, both internally and externally. In other words the physical structure of the human body is inseparable from the external world. Yin and yang oppositions include light and dark, heaven and earth, day and night, hot and cold, male and female, fast and slow, fire and water, and sun and moon.

Another important aspect of Chinese philosophy is the theory of the five phases (wu xing). The five phases are earth, metal, water, wood and fire. These are not an absolute correlation to the five elements more familiar in western tradition but rather a group of dynamic relations which occur between the individual elements which progress in five phases.

The most important aspect or concept of Chinese medicine is qi – where the body is influenced by internal functions and external factors to obtain and maintain a state of health or well being. Sometimes qi is referred to as energy but it is a very broad term and there are different types of qi in the body depending on their source, location and function. Qi, along with essence and spirit, make up the three treasures. Essence comes from the parents and is a fundamental source of human physiological processes, and spirit, which comes from heaven, controls a person's radiance and alertness. Finally in Chinese medicine the mind and body are not separate entities and they interact with, and depend on, each other.

According to Chinese medicine the body is divided into 12 organ functions. These organs are divided into the viscera, which has six solid organs or zang, and the bowels which has another six hollow organs or fu. The heart, lungs, liver, spleen, kidneys and pericardium are the viscera, and the small and large intestines, stomach, urinary bladder and the 'triple burner' comprise the bowels. The 'triple burner' does not have an exact physical form and so its purpose, form and location have been frequently debated. However, these organs do not always correlate precisely to their western equivalent as function, rather than form, is more important to Chinese philosophy.

The organs are paired and have yin and yang relationships. Each viscera and bowel has a channel which runs through the organ, across the surface of the body and connects to the related organ. There are 12 primary channels and eight extraordinary vessels. The channels are organised in six yin-yang pairings and qi flows along them. Along the 12 primary channels, and two of the others, there are 361 acupuncture points. There are also a large number of other points which have been identified. The Chinese term for point is zue, which means hole. The holes are where qi can be influenced by the insertion of needles.

Application and practice
All illnesses are caused by a disturbance of qi according to Chinese medicine. There are three categories of disease which are identified by their cause: external, internal and causes which are neither internal nor external. There are six external environmental causes or evils: wind, fire, cold, damp, heat and dry. The seven internal causes or damages are joy, anxiety, fear, sorrow, anger, thought and fright. The third category of causes include excessive sexual behaviour, dietary imbalance, fatigue, trauma and parasitic infection. The effect of wind and cold can be seen in the type of symptoms associated with colds such as aching muscles, fever, headache and sore throat. Internal symptoms caused by the seven damages

include mental or emotional states which affect the physical body.

Diagnosis using Chinese medicine involves four areas: inspection, smelling and listening, interrogation and palpation or touch. The patient should be assessed visually in relation to their spirit, form and bearing. The tongue is examined for colour, markings and coatings. Moistness or dryness are also important diagnostic features. The second component is smelling and listening. Listening to the breathing, speech and other internal sounds and smelling of the breath, body aromas and excreta. Interrogation involves the process of asking the patient for their medical history. These questions should include ones about bodily sensations such as hot and cold, dry and wet, thirst, hunger, previous illnesses and treatments. The final stage is touch, or palpation, which includes a general palpation of the body and acupuncture points as well the pulse.

Once the examination is complete the practitioner makes a plan of the disease and its treatment. There should be a gathering of symptoms and signs of the affect of the illness on various aspects of the patients body, organs and channels which aid the diagnostic process and. Once the location of the problem is identified it is assessed using eight principles: yin, yang, hot, cold, exterior, interior, vacuity or deficiency and repletion or excess. The next stage is the use of allopathic therapy. In other words therapy which attacks the condition by opposing it, or treatment by opposition. The disease is either treated from its root, by elimination of evil factors and restoration of harmony.

Therapeutic methods include acupuncture, moxibustion, cupping and bleeding, massage, qigong, herbal medicine and diet. Acupuncture regulates qi and the blood flow. When channels are blocked illness occurs and acupuncture removes the blockages. Moxibustion is the burning of the dried and powdered leaves of the artemesia vulgaris on or near the skin. Again the theory is that the burning will release the blockage and restore the movement of qi. Those diseases which are best treated by these methods are those of the respiratory system such as colds, asthma, bronchitis, rhinitus, sinusitis and tonsillitis; disorders of the eye; mouth; digestive system, and musculoskeletal and neuralgic problems including headache, paralysis following stroke, sciatica, osteoarthritis and bladder dysfunction.

Cupping and bleeding are important to Chinese medicine and they can be used either together, along with with other treatments or separately. Cupping involves placing a heated glass or cup over the skin to form a vacuum. This brings blood to the surface and increases local circulation of blood and lymph fluids. Bleeding drains a channel, or removes heat from the body, but only involves very small amounts of blood. The term Tui Na means pushing and pulling and includes a method of massage, acupressure and manipulation. The techniques which are used are kneading, rubbing, pulling, pushing and they are applied intensively to a limited area of the body. Is is most useful for orthopaedic conditions but can also be used for asthma, chronic digestive problems and painful periods. It can increase the range of movement in a joint and so can be used with acupuncture or pressure can be applied to the points if the use of needles is unacceptable.

Qigong covers all aspects of the control of qi by exercise, breathing and mental attitude. It incorporates Daoist and Buddhist principles of meditation and although it is part of the training for a practitioner of Chinese medicine, patients themselves can be taught to carry out routines and practices which are helpful for their conditions.

Herbal medicine is an important part of

Chinese medicine and culture. The material used for medicines does not only include herbs but animals and minerals as well. The numbers of substances recorded in the *Encyclopaedia of Traditional Chinese Medicine* is 5, 767. The prescribing of medicinal recipes and remedies is very complex and should only be done by a fully trained practitioner.

The final component of Chinese medicine is dietary therapy. Many foods which are used as part of a therapy are also part of the regular diet eaten by most people and reflect the cultural awareness of the importance of the harmony of yin and yang.

CHIROPRACTIC

History and origins

Spinal manipulation has been practised for centuries in many cultures. Some of the great medical authorities such as Hippocrates and Galen used spinal manipulation not only to help specific spinal problems but also other seemingly unrelated problems. During the renaissance in Europe, when medical practice was based on the works of these ancients, manipulation was used by surgeons and physicians. In later generations certain families handed-down manipulative knowledge and skills and were often known as bone-setters.

Daniel David Palmer established the first school of chiropractic in America in 1895. Palmer had cured a deaf man, Harvey Lillard. Lillard had suffered acute back pain for many years and Palmer, noticing a spinal misalignment or what he called a subluxation, administered a manipulative readjustment. Lillard was not only relieved of his back pain but was also able to hear for the first time in years. Unfortunately Palmer had not found a cure for deafness, however he had relieved Lillard's's musculoskeletal pain and disability and restored internal organ function and balance.

Palmer founded his system of treatment which was based on the principle that all diseases are caused by spinal misalignment and that they are cured by manual manipulation of the vertebrae. Like osteopathy no drugs are used in chiropractic therapy.

There was much opposition to chiropractic therapy, especially from orthodox allopathic medical authorities, and some of the early practitioners, including Palmer himself, were jailed for carrying out their therapies. However, by the 1990s spinal manipulation therapy for low back pain was finally recognised as offering increased, and rapid, recovery. Chiropractic also offered treatment combined with, or without, the use of medication. The other main area where chiropractic treatment is used is in relation to muscle-tension headaches.

Theory and principles
Chiropractic emphasises the principle that the human body possesses its own natural healing

potential. It also stresses that addressing the cause of any condition or illness is preferable to simply suppressing its obvious physical manifestations. Suppression of symptoms through chemical medication can compromise the body's own natural self-healing ability. Spinal manipulation should be one of the first lines of attack rather than treatment of symptoms by medication. Also important are diet and exercise. A balanced diet is crucial to good health. Regular exercise maintains proper body function. Since structure and function are closely linked, and any internal structural distortion can cause functional problems. Spinal misalignment can also lead to a variety of functional problems. Chiropractors believe that the site of the problem is not necessarily the site of the cause. Restoration and maintenance of body function is controlled and influenced by the nervous system. Spinal misalignment can cause malfunction through neurological effect. In other words spinal disorders can cause problems elsewhere in the body such as the arms, legs or hips, as well as spinal symptoms themselves such as sciatica or lumbago. It is also possible that unrelated symptoms such as migraine or asthma may result from spinal problems.

Although chiropractic relieves musculoskeletal pain its main principles of therapy do not address pain relief in general. The main focus is addressing the structural and functional imbalance which may have caused the pain.

By the 1980s the simple spinal misalignment theory was replaced by the more complex theory of intervertebral motion and segmental dysfunction. This theory proposes that loss of joint mobility and rigid fixation, rather than misalignment, causes the dysfunction. Segmental dysfunction is identified by point tenderness or altered pain threshold to pressure when applied to specific points, contraction or tension within the spinal muscles and loss of normal movement.

Application and practice - Examination
The patient is examined and questioned about specific details of their case history. Painful or tender joints are checked for any dysfunction, as well as an evaluation of the painful area in context of the whole body. X-rays may be used to help make detailed diagnosis of any bone disease, fractures or arthritis. The chiropractor should rule out any conditions which contraindicate manipulation such as cancers, bone and joint infection, acute fractures and dislocations,

Chiropractic

rheumatoid conditions or diseases of the spine.

Treatment

High-velocity, low-amplitude (HVLA) thrust adjustment is the most common form of chiropractic manipulation. HVLA is achieved by moving a joint through its normal range of movement, putting local pressure on bony prominences and then carrying out a quick, low-amplitude thrust. This low-amplitude thrust is often associated with a clicking sound which indicates the joint moving to the furthest extent of its normal range of movement. When this procedure is correctly administered it should be painless.

If the low-amplitude thrust manipulation is contraindicated then non-realignment procedures can be used, these include trigger point therapy, joint mobilising and massage.

Some patients may feel some residual discomfort after treatment, although others may experience immediate pain relief. Some conditions will require several treatments, particularly those conditions which have been chronic or longstanding rather than of recent onset.

There is some research currently being carried

out to investigate the potential benefits from chiropractic therapy for other non-muscle or joint conditions. It may be proven, and accepted, in the future that disorders such as painful periods, high blood pressure, infantile colic, vertigo and tinnitus will be able to be successfully treated by chiropractors.

At the moment there is only a small number of chiropractors in the United Kingdom but this is increasing, as is the level of contact and cooperation between allopathic practitioners and chiropractors. Referrals to chiropractors for muscle and joint problems is increasing.

CHUA KA

Chua Ka is another form of deep-tissue massage which helps relieve tension and muscular aches. Although it is not well known about at the moment interest in chua ka, along with other oriental practice, is growing. Those who use chua ka believe that it helps those who are tense and stressed.

Like the other forms of Oriental massage there are few contraindications but those who have a serious long term medical condition should check before trying it.

History and origins
Chua ka originated with Mongolian soldiers during their preparations before battle. They performed manipulations to purge fear and trauma, in order that they could fight effectively that day without past experiences interfering with the abilities.

Application and practice

chua ka is a deep-tissue massage technique which can be self-administered or performed on other people. The theory is that unpleasant experiences and emotional problems cause muscle tension. Those who practise chua ka believe that different areas of the body are affected by different emotional stresses. By performing chua ka to a particular part of the body tension is released. As the muscle tension disappears so does the corresponding emotional problem.

There are three different techniques to chua ka. First, firm hand pressure is used to massage the muscles. The second stage involves the use of a flat massage stick or ka stick. The ka stick is used in the same way as the fingers are used during shiatsu. The third technique uses sweeping, vertical strokes called skin rolling. All three techniques help loosen the body and assist relaxation.

COLOUR THERAPY

Closely related to chakra balancing is colour therapy where colour is used to treat mental, emotional and physical problems. It is also related to light therapy, although rather than general broad spectrum light specific colours are used.

Colour treatment is useful for those suffering chronic pain, skin problems, tiredness and aching muscles, rheumatism, arthritis, headaches and migraines, jaundice and visual disturbances. It can also help those who are stressed, agitated, depressed or tired.

History and origins

The use of colour to treat illness was used by Egyptians. Healing buildings were built which had rooms painted the different colours of the rainbow. Patients were put into different rooms depending on their specific illnesses or complaints. Greeks also used colour as part of their therapies, as did the Chinese and ayurvedic traditions of the east. In India each chakra corresponds to a particular colour.

Theory and principles

Light is a form of radiant energy but it consists of different wave lengths some of which are not visible to the naked eye. We see only those waves which fall into the visible spectrum – violet has the shortest wave and red the longest. Isaac Newton discovered that a beam of sunlight shone through a prism separated into a range of colours like those seen in a rainbow. There are other invisible wavelengths of light such as ultraviolet, microwaves and X-rays which have been shown to affect the body but there is much controversy about whether visible light can affect the body as well.

Day colours are red, orange and yellow and have an energising affect, whereas night colours – blue, indigo and violet – are calming and restorative.

Although scientific evidence is sparse colours are certainly associated with moods and feelings. It has been shown that some colours have a relaxing effect and others stimulate and energise. Some colours – such as black – are depressing, red and orange excite, while blue and green are

Colour therapy

calming and relaxing.

Some practitioners use blue light to treat arthritis and infant jaundice. Intermittent red or blue light has been used to treat migraines. Use of intermittent light has also been shown to influence athletic energy – red light resulted in quick energy surges whereas blue light resulted in a steady energy level.

Application and practice

Colour therapy is used by colouring the environment either by paint or by the use of coloured light bulbs. The following are some basic applications for different coloured rooms or light.

Red – associated with skin conditions, circulation, energy, anaemia, muscle aches, arthritis and rheumatism.

Orange – useful for respiratory conditions such as asthma, muscle cramps and spasms, digestive disorders and general bodily harmony.

Yellow – helps constipation, arthritis and can stimulate energy.

Green – associated with a general feeling of well-being and harmony.

Blue-green – helps stress and fever.

Turquoise – relieves headaches, swelling, itching, burns and sunburn.

Blue – helps treat fever, stress, high blood pressure and sleep disorders.
Indigo – is associated with treating ear and eye problems.
Violet – helps cramps and spasms, high blood pressure and bladder problems.
Magenta – has a general stimulating effect.

Mood can also be influenced by the colour of clothes worn by an individual. The following is a short list of some recognised associations between colour and mood.
Red – associated with strength and courage.
Yellow – associated with happiness and communication.
Green – associated with stability.
Blue – associated with peace and calm.
Orange – associated with sexual energy and self-esteem.
Purple – associated with higher intellectual ability and position.
Black – associated with self-effacement.
White – associated with focus and clarity.

CRYSTAL THERAPY

Crystal therapy uses gemstones and quartz crystals to promote wellbeing and health and treat ill-health.

It is useful for headaches, digestive problems, ear and eye troubles, chest and breathing problems and glandular disturbances. Those suffering from stress, anger, depression and sadness, anxiety, sleep disturbances, poor memory and low self esteem may also be helped using crystals.

Crystals are often used in conjunction with meditation and low lighting and a warm, safe environment are important.

History and origins
The use of gemstones and crystals has a long history. Egyptians used them in religious ceremonies as well as for healing. In particular pearls were thought to aid immortality. Buddhist and Hindu writings contain references to the

mystical powers of gems. Native Americans used gems and crystals in healing rituals.

Certain metals were thought to have particular healing powers – especially gold and silver and those who were skilled in their use were often perceived to have special healing knowledge and skills. Specific gems were also thought to relate to specific conditions. Opals were believed to prevent blindness and a necklace of amber beads was often worn to protect against other eye conditions. The use of crushed stones and jewels was an expensive method of preparing medicine so a cheaper method was to soak the stone in a dilute alcohol solution. After some time the gem would be removed and kept for later use and the alcohol solution used to make medicines.

Theory and principles

Those who believe in crystal therapy believe that they have electromagnetic energy and emit vibrations which affect the body and the mind. There is no specific scientific evidence to support the claims that crystals help but many people have personal anecdotal accounts of the benefits which have been obtained from the use of crystals.

Crystal therapy

Application and practice

A crystal therapist can give advice about specific gems and stones to use for particular conditions, but most people consult books about the subject and try different stones themselves to see what effect they have.

Crystals can be used in a number of ways. They can be used as jewellery, carried loose in pockets or clothing, placed as ornaments around the house or placed on parts of the body when lying or sitting. Often crystals are placed on energy points – chakras or meridians – and a meditation exercise is used at the same time.

Before using a crystal it is important to clear it by washing it in sea or salt water, burying it underground, holding it under running water or passing it through smoke or flame. Any of these procedures will remove any bad vibrations or effects from people who have previously been in contact with the stone.

Some of the most commonly used crystals and their characteristics are:

Adventurine – balances emotions.

Amber – helps express emotions.

Amethyst – purifies and clear thoughts.

Aquamarine – brings peace of mind and relieves anxiety.

Azurite – clears the mind.

Bloodstone – promotes physical healing.

Boji stone – heals and balances.

Carnelian – regenerates and helps tiredness.

Citrine – help depression.

Clear quartz – helps focus the mind.

Fluorite – clears the mind.

Garnet – invigorates.

Hematite – releases stress and energy.

Jade – cleanses and nurtures.

Kinzite – opens the heart.

Lapis lazuli – calms, strengthens and gives courage.

Lepidolite – promotes peace and tranquillity.

Malachite – balances love and patience.

Moldavite – stimulates the brain.

Moonstone – increases psychic awareness.

Obsidian – calms the emotions.

Onyx – reduces negative energy.

Orange coral – protects.

Peridot – helps release anger and increase

spiritual awareness.

Rhodonite – helps self-expression.

Selenite – helps concentration.

Smoky quartz – stimulates dreams.

Sodalite – helps metabolic balance.

Sugilite – increases spiritual awareness.

Tiger's eye – helps decision making and concentration.

Turquoise – protects and increases the imagination and creativity.

DO-IN

Do-In – which is pronounced dough-in – is a simple form of oriental exercise and self-massage.

It is useful for muscle and joint pain and stiffness, and it can also relieve or prevent stress, tension and insomnia. People of any age can participate, but they must be active and not out of condition. Do-In should be avoided after heavy meals.

Do-In is still relatively unknown in the west but it is starting to be included in literature about alternative healing techniques.

History, origins and theory
Do-In is part of the oriental holistic tradition. It is part of a complete philosophy that also includes diet, breathing exercises, meditation and other physical exercise.

It developed in Japan where it was the custom to make important decisions in the early morning. The fresh air and new day cleared the mind of confusing thoughts and the body and soul would be stimulated and in harmony. It is based on the concept of meridians and so has some connections with shiatsu. The best time to practice Do-In is in the morning although it can be done at any time during the day.

Application and practice

The techniques of Do-In are relatively simple and adaptable. Most of the massage techniques are the same as in other procedures: kneading, pounding, pressing and tapping.

Before starting it is best to do some warming-up exercises to reduce stiffness and increase suppleness. A whole-body massage starting with the face and neck, working down towards the feet, will stimulate the circulation. Deep breathing exercises at the same time are also beneficial. The massage can start with light tapping all over the head. Then massage the scalp as if washing the hair. The ears should be massaged next. With three fingers press the rim of the ear, pushing it against the head. Then massage the whole ear with the thumb and index finger. The face should be covered with the palms of the hands against the cheeks and then rubbed up and down briskly.

As the massage progresses down towards the

Do-in

feet sit on the ground with the knees up. Grasp them and start rocking. Sit up and, with the soles of the feet touching and knees apart, hold the toes/feet for a couple of minutes. It is also suggested that the feet are rubbed against each other briskly until they tingle. For the back and bottom kneel on the floor and rest back on the heels. With loose fists pound the back and bottom, starting as high as possible, work down and then work back up again. This should be done several times.

Later, if there has been a lot of sitting, it is helpful to massage the back and shoulders. Start at the lower back and press with both thumbs on the indentation near the bottom of the spine. Press the spot several times. The whole area can then be massaged using the fingers. Then stand up and stretch as much as possible, roll the shoulders up to the ears and contract the shoulder muscles. Drop them back and let the muscles relax. This can be done several times. Next drop one shoulder down and contract and relax the muscles on the higher shoulder a few times, keeping the lower shoulder relaxed. Reverse the positions and repeat. Then pound each shoulder with a loose fist and knead the top of the shoulders with fingers and palms. Finally, tall stretches and shoulder shrugs should compete the routine. This procedure should be carried out kneeling on the floor but it can be done sitting at a chair. For those who sit at desks for most of the day it can be carried out at regular intervals throughout the day and can help prevent backache. Even if the whole routine is not carried out kneading the lower back and the stretches and shoulder shrugs are useful.

For a gastric or stomach exercise stand near a wall. Place one hand, palm down, high up on the wall. With the other hand grip the foot opposite to the raised arm and raise it to the height of the bottom. Then stretch the neck and head backwards, away from the wall. Holding this position inhale and exhale deeply twice, then relax. The repeat the exercise in reverse.

An exercise which stimulates the large intestine meridian involves standing upright. With the thumbs linked behind the back inhale. During exhalation place the arms outwards and upwards behind the back. Finally lean forwards from the hips and then stand upright.

To stimulate the bladder meridian sit on the floor with the legs straight out in front. The toes should be tensed upright. Stretch the arms above the head and inhale deeply. After exhaling bend forwards from the shoulders, arms in front, towards the feet. The toes should then be grasped and the position held for three deep breaths. Then repeat the whole procedure.

For the liver sit upright on the floor, with the legs as far apart as possible. Inhale and pass the arms down the right leg to hold the foot. Hold this stretched position for two deep breaths then repeat for the opposite leg.

A cardiac exercise which helps the whole circulation involves sitting on the floor with the feet touching and knees bent. Cross the hands and grasp the opposite knee then bend the body forwards as if pushing the knees down to the floor.

After all the routines have been carried out lie flat on the floor, legs apart and arms stretched with palms up. Lift the head slightly and then relax and let it touch the floor. Shake the head and body to loosen the legs, arms and neck. Then lie quietly with the eyes shut for a few minutes.

HEALING TOUCH

Healing touch is based on the concept of healing energies. It is a combination of traditional techniques and new methods and theories about healing energy. It can relieve emotional and physical symptoms. Most therapies are based on the theory that by applying pressure on one area another part of the body will be influenced as well. For example acupressure uses the same points as acupuncture but fingers instead of needles are used. Most, although not all, forms of healing touch have their basis in Oriental healing practices. Some methods rely on the sense of touch by the healer to identify the patient's energy flow. Other systems rely on self-healing by using meditation to identify personal energy flows.

The main systems of healing touch are:
- *healing touch*
- *reflexology*
- *acupressure*

- *shiatsu massage*
- *external qigong*

History and origins

Healing touch, pranic or qigong healing, using energy flows has a multicultural background. Indian, Chinese, Japanese, Thai and Hawaiian cultures all had a tradition of healing touch. In India it was referred to as prana or pranic healing, in China as ch'i, in Japan as ki and Thailand as qi. Hawaiians referred to the term mana. Mesmer called it animal magnetism. Western cultures, particularly those in industrialised countries, have no concept or language for healing energy.

Healing touch and therapeutic touch

Healing touch and therapeutic touch are two recognised methods employed in western societies. The method of healing actually involves very little touch as the hands are passed over the body some inches away from the body. The responses or sensations that both the healer and patient report are therefore little to do with physical pressure and suggests that there is some other energy responsible. Although many techniques are developed intuitively, and are dependent on the personal and emotional balance

Healing touch

of the healer, some specific movements are used for back pain, to reduce the effects of drugs and anaesthesia, and to help relieve depression and increase relaxation. The difference in the principle of healing touch is that both the patient and the healer are equally important.

When a patient is treated the healing touch practitioner needs to assess the patient's energetic state. The healer will identify depressions, obstructions, holes, and hot and cold spots around the patient. These reflect problems within the patient's life – emotional or physical. The aim of healing touch is to free or unblock obstructions in order to permit a free energy flow. Although healing touch can be carried out by a practitioner the patient themselves are encouraged to learn to interpret and be sensitive to their own energy currents through meditation, relaxation, visualisation and counselling.

Uses of healing touch

Healing touch is especially useful in psychiatric care, children's nursing, maternity units, patient's undergoing treatment for cancer and for HIV and AIDS, and in intensive care situations. It can help reduce stress, pain, swelling, temperatures, depression and tiredness.

REFLEXOLOGY

Reflexology, or zone therapy, is the diagnosis and treatment of conditions by massaging and applying pressure to certain parts of the body, usually the feet. Although its origins may be older William Fitzgerald, an American, identified ten energy channels around the human body. The channels, or zones, ended at the hands and feet and when pressure was applied to certain parts of the feet, or hands, pain felt elsewhere would be improved. Most organs have a pressure point on the feet or hands and the massaging of the particular pressure point relieves the energy blockage which may be causing the problem. The pressure also helps relax muscles and stimulates the body's own natural ability to heal. Reflexology is closely related to acupressure and acupuncture.

Although it is not a therapy for any specific condition it can be particularly useful in relieving the symptoms of chronic pain, stress, insomnia, stomach and digestive disorders, arthritis and asthma. As it relieves symptoms it also helps with breathing exercises and relaxation. Reflexology cannot be used in conditions which require surgery. It is not appropriate in heart conditions, osteoporosis and thyroid problems. As pressure is applied to a specific point a sensation may be created elsewhere in the body.

History and origins

Traditionally oriental or eastern healing theories included massaging of the hands and feet to affect internal organs and muscles. The technique may be 5000 years old but it was not until 1913 that William Fitzgerald introduced zone therapy to the United States of America. His ten zone theory identified bioelectrical energy which flowed from the zones to reflex points on the feet and hands. Although they differed slightly from Chinese meridians and energy flows, both systems have similar philosophies in that the body's internal energy force can be manipulated by touch.

Some 25 years later Eunice Ingham, who was a physiotherapist, identified the feet as being the most important areas because they were more sensitive than the hands. She mapped out the whole body and related it to specific points on the feet. Ingham later established an institute of

Healing touch – reflexology

reflexology where she taught and trained other practitioners. Ingham's method it still popular today although another system devised by Laura Norman is also used. Although the feet are still very important some reflexologists do perform therapy using the hands and other areas of the body.

In the 1960s Robert St John developed another variation of reflexology. He identified a reflex-point chart of the foot which had the spine following the line along the inside side of the foot from the toe to the heel. He then related the nine month gestation period to nine spinal points. His theory was that the unborn child was affected by emotional events during the mother's pregnancy. Different hormone levels at times of crisis would affect the foetus, which would be stored in the spinal reflexes to affect the person in later life. St John's method, called the Metamorphic Technique, attempted to relieve the prenatal traumas which contributed to later ill health and disease.

Theory and principles

Some reflexologists only use reflexology but many use it as part of a holistic approach to healing and use it along with other healing techniques. There is little scientific proof to support the benefits claimed by reflexologists but there is anecdotal evidence that the practice does work. Some suggest it is the relaxation which is as helpful as the reflexology itself. However, all agree that stroking and applying pressure to particular points removes blockages in energy flows. According to some reflexology stimulates the sensory receptors in the nerve fibres and impulses then disperse energy through the whole nervous system. Another theory suggests that the manipulation breaks up and dissolves uric acid deposits which have accumulated in the extremities. A third interpretation believes that endorphins, natural pain-relieving chemicals, are released into the blood stream during the massaging and stimulation.

All these theories may be correct but at the moment have not been proved scientifically. What is certainly true is that the treatment is relaxing and that during relaxation the circulation of blood and lymphatic fluid is improved. The increase in the circulation of blood increases oxygen flow to body cells as well as helps the removal of toxic waste.

Healing touch – reflexology

Application and practice

The reflexologist should encourage the patient to breath deeply in order to encourage relaxation during treatment sessions. The treatment may be carried out lying down or sitting up. Initially both feet should be massaged gently then the reflexologist will work down through the reflex points on each foot. The feet and toes can be rubbed, moved up and down and rotated and the therapist will also stroke and apply deep pressure.

There should be no pain but occasionally some people do experience a sharp, stabbing pain. There is often an associated tingling in another part of the body. The tingling should be felt in the area which relates to the reflex point being treated.

For general relaxation weekly sessions of thirty minutes to one hour are recommended. If a specific condition or symptom is to be treated then more frequent sessions may be required. The length of treatment can vary – some people feel improvement after one or two sessions, others may take longer.

Reflexology can be tried on a self-help basis or with the help of a partner. The foot should be held in both hands, with the fingers at the top and the thumbs on the sole. Then, pressing firmly, slide both thumbs from the outside edge of the foot across the sole and back. This should be done working down the length of the foot. The foot should then be twisted gently, then flexed at the ankle. Next the foot should be held with one hand and ball of the foot pressed with the thumb. The pressure should then be released and the thumb rotated on the point. The next stage involves pressing, releasing and rotating in turn, starting with each of the toes and working down the length of the foot to the ankle. The whole foot should then be twisted, gently, by holding it in both hands and moving the hands in opposite directions. The basic relaxation stage is then completed by gently slapping the foot from one hand to the other.

Professional reflexologists carry out the above procedure with added finger movements and techniques for specific parts of the body. Simple self-treatment for relaxation purposes does not require these extra techniques. If specific problems need treated then further knowledge about the reflex points and their related body parts is necessary. The reflex points on the left relate to those areas on the left of the body, and those on the right relate to body parts on the right. A general list of reflex points includes:

Healing touch – reflexology

- *Toes relate to the head, brain and sinuses.*
- *Joint where toes and foot meet corresponds to the ears and eyes.*
- *The ball of the foot relates to the lungs and heart.*
- *The arch of the foot is connected to the internal organs like the kidneys and colon.*
- *The heel relates to the sciatic nerve and pelvic area.*

The bone on the arch of the foot corresponds to the spine.

A more complete chart of the foot used by professionals is much more specific and complex than this list.

Reflex points found on the rest of the body include the abdominal, chest, head and ear areas. The abdominal reflex usually indicates a problem in this area. The chest reflex relates to a number of major organs in the body. Those on the head correspond to the stomach, kidneys, spleen and pancreas. Another important area is the area at the back of the neck where the brain joins the spine. If this area is massaged nervous tension is relieved and energy is released. The reflex points on the ears are difficult to locate but it has been reported that ear conditions such as tinnitus have been relieved using reflexology on the ears.

These reflex points can be stimulated in the same way as those on the feet and hands using circular massage and pressure followed by release.

Some general uses of reflexology - The digestive system

Gastric or stomach problems can be treated by reflexology either using the abdominal reflex or on the feet or hands. Other associated organs like the liver, gall bladder and colon can also be treated. The abdominal point should be pressed then released three times in order to stimulate the reflex.

On the hands the soft tissue between the thumb and forefinger on the left hand can be worked with the right thumb for a few minutes. This can then be reversed and the right hand worked by the left one although most relief will be gained from working the left hand as the stomach lies on the left.

Massaging the instep of the left foot can relieve digestive problems. Both hand and feet reflexes can be worked for stomach, colon, liver and kidney disorders. The thyroid is another important reflex to stimulate as it will help regulate the body functions.

Other gastric problems like ulcers may be

Healing touch – reflexology

helped by reflexology. The feet can be massaged and the stomach and duodenum reflexes worked on, as well as the liver and endocrine glands.

Heart and circulation problems

The heart can be stimulated and maintained by massaging the related reflex points. It is also useful to exercise the left arm using side-to-side movements. The neck and chest muscles can then also be massaged to relieve tension.

A useful diagnostic test can be done by applying quite hard pressure to the pad of the left thumb. If this hurts at the top then it may indicate a constriction in the cardiac vessels which could affect blood supply. If it hurts at the bottom then the arteries may be congested. If the whole area is too sensitive to touch then there is the possibility of a heart attack.

Many blood and circulation problems can be helped by massage. The endocrine reflexes on the feet should be worked, as well as those for the circulation system in general.

Conditions such as angina, hypertension, palpitations and varicose veins may be helped by reflexology.

Respiratory and lung problems

Asthma may be helped by reflexology. An important respiratory reflex is at the back of the neck, at the base of the collar bones. If this point is pressed with a downward movement for a few seconds some relief from asthmatic symptoms may be felt. There are other reflex points on either side of the spine in the shoulder area. On the feet the brain, endocrine, the lungs and the circulatory reflex points can also be worked to provide relief. The reflex points for the lungs are particularly important. The massage point for the diaphragm is at the point where the instep joins that ball of the foot. Asthmatic symptoms can be helped if this area is worked. During an asthma attack thumbs can be placed on these reflexes to help alleviate the symptoms.

The stimulation of adrenaline and cortisone is also important in controlling respiration. Therefore another important reflex to stimulate is the adrenal one which produces adrenaline and cortisone. The adrenal reflex is located in the middle of the sole and the palm.

Other chest conditions such as bronchitis and emphysema can be helped by massaging the reflex points for the brain, endocrine system, lungs and diaphragm, neck and shoulders as well as the

Healing touch – reflexology

heart and circulatory system.

Chest infections – colds and coughs – can be treated using the above reflexes. In the case of colds working the sinus and facial reflexes is also useful.

The endocrine glands

These glands release hormones into the blood or lymphatic system. The major glands are thyroid, parathyroid, pineal, pituitary, pancreas, thymus, adrenal and gonads. Endocrine glands control growth, daily rhythms, metabolism, immunity, heart and breathing, sugar levels and reproductive activity. Any imbalance in the endocrine system is serious and restoration of equilibrium is very important. In general massaging of the brain reflex is important, as is the pituitary gland reflex. These reflexes should be gently massaged with thumbs or fingers for a few seconds, pressure should then be applied which should be released slowly.

The liver and spleen

The liver is an important organ which controls internal metabolism. It is the largest organ in the body and is found in the right side of the abdominal cavity. It converts glucose to glycogen which is stored as a food reserve. Excess amino acids are converted into urea for excretion. Poisons are also broken down in the liver and red blood cells are recycled to remove iron. The liver also stores vitamins.

The liver reflexes are found on large areas on the sole of the right foot and on the palm of the right hand. The general procedure involves massaging either area with the left thumb.

The gall bladder is also associated with the liver. Its reflex is located at the bottom of the liver reflex on the sole and palm. There is another gall bladder reflex on the body just below the ribs on the right side. The spleen is also associated with the liver but its reflex is found on the left palm or sole, just below the heart reflex.

Kidneys and bladder

These reflexes are situated just off centre on both soles and palms. They are near the pancreas and stomach. The bladder reflex is near the base of the palm, at the wrist, and on the inside edge of the soles near the heel. Other kidney reflexes are found at the side of the body at the waistline, between the hip and ribs, as well as on the face just below the eyes.

Healing touch – reflexology

Back pain and other skeletal problems
The spinal reflex on the feet is found running from the base of the big toe to the heel. If this line is worked any tender or sensitive points can be found and stimulated. The top of the line is associated with the top of the spine, near the shoulders.

Reflexologists often work the muscles in the legs to help back pain. The back of the thigh can be massaged by pulling and pressing actions, from the top of the thigh down to the knee.

There are specific reflexes found on the feet and hands which relate to the shoulders, hips and neck. At the same time as the skeletal reflexes the endocrine, digestive and circulatory systems should also be worked in order to benefit the whole body.

Arthritis
Arthritis is an extremely painful and debilitating disease. Massage of the reflex points for the most affected areas is important to relieve discomfort. However, massage of all the body reflexes is also helpful to achieve total comfort and relief. The endocrine system is particularly important in the treatment of arthritis. By stimulation of the adrenal organ cortisone is produced naturally

which can help relief pain. The adrenal gland is stimulated at the reflex point found on the lower back, between the first and second lumber vertebrae.

Stress and tension
An additional benefit of reflexology is the overall state of relaxation which is achieved. A feeling of wellbeing is generated and tension is released. Deep breathing can help, as well as clasping the hands. Massage of the endocrine system can help restore hormonal balance and reduce tension, as can massaging of the reflex related to the neck and spine. Controlling the heart rate by massaging the cardiac reflexes can help reduce stress.

The reproductive system
The ovarian reflexes are found on the outer side of the foot, just below the ankle. Points are also found on the hands just beyond the wrist. The reflex points related to the breasts are on the outer edges of both hands and feet, just below the little finger and toe. The uterine reflex is just below the wrist on the inner aspect of the arm or in the inside of the foot , just below the ankle.

The male reflexes are located in the same place as the female ones. Therefore the reflexes related to the penis is found at the same location as the uterine ones and the testes situated at the site of the ovarian reflexes. The prostate gland reflex is found near the penis reflex. The endocrine gland reflexes are also important in relation to the reproduction system.

Reflexology is useful for many menstrual conditions such as amenorrhoea (absence of menstruation), fibroids, leucorrhoea (yellow/white vaginal discharge), premenstrual tension, endometriosis, painful periods, excessive menstrual bleeding and menopausal symptoms.

Immune problems

The lymphatic system is important in controlling the body's immune response. Swellings occur in lymph nodes at various points on the body, particularly the neck, groin and armpit. Since both the endocrine and lymphatic systems are important in maintaining good bodily health and balance then reflexology can be useful in restoring this balance.

There are lymph reflex points on the back of the hands, found just over the wrists, and on the top of the feet. These can be worked in association with those for the endocrine gland, the circulation and the liver.

ACUPRESSURE

The methods and movement are quite different from those of Swedish massage.

By rubbing an affected or sore area blood flow is increased which aids healing. By stimulating the circulation oxygen is increased and toxic waste is removed. The Chinese formulated the theories and principles of acupuncture and acupressure 3000 years ago. It was noticed that particular conditions were affected by pressure to different parts of the body. These pressure points were catalogued and related to each other, and twelve pathways or meridians on each side of the body were identified. By applying pressure to these pathways blockages, which contributed to ill health, were removed.

The Chinese introduced acupuncture to the Japanese and in the eighteenth century the Japanese introduced a new technique which did not use needles and combined acupuncture with a form of massage. This version would later become known as Shiatsu. Although sometimes shiatsu and acupressure are used interchangeably they are not exactly the same.

Acupressure can be self-administered, unlike acupuncture, and it can be used to maintain good health as well as to treat disease or restore health. As it is non-invasive it is very safe compared to those which use drugs or other more dangerous techniques.

Theory and principles

Acupressure enhances the body's own healing systems which not only restores health but also helps prevent illness by improving general energy levels. The pressure regulates qi, the energy which flows along the pathways or meridians. Meridians are related to the internal organs or systems of the body, like the stomach, the liver or the endocrine system. However, there are four meridians which are exceptions to this, namely 'the conception', the 'governor', the 'pericardium' and the 'triple heater'.

Pressure points located in specific parts of the body are massaged using the thumb or fingertip. Professional acupressure therapists sometimes use their knuckles or elbows to massage the points but for self-treatment fingers and thumbs are sufficient. The pressure applied should not be either too gentle or too hard, and should certainly not cause any pain or discomfort. Pressure should be applied for three to seven seconds, and should be repeated no more than three or four times. For some conditions relief may be immediate, but other, more chronic conditions, may take longer to improve.

Application and practice

During a professional consultation a general examination should be carried out as well as a discussion about diet and lifestyle. The pulse should be taken as well as a history of the specific condition. The acupressure therapist does not use oils or any other special equipment, and a session may last up to one hour. As the pressure is applied the patient may feel several sensations. Some points may be sore or tender, or some slight discomfort or pain felt may be felt.

An acupressure session should be carried out in a warm, relaxed environment. Loose comfortable clothing should be worn and the patient should lie on a firm mattress or a rug on the floor. In the first instance the whole body should be pressed to identify the sensitive areas. Any tender areas indicate the internal problem and these should be massaged rapidly. Discomfort should be minimal and should pass quickly, and there should be no pain. Particular care should be taken when massaging the stomach, face and joints. If a young child or baby is being massaged then the pressure should be more gentle.

Some general acupressure treatments
Colds and coughs

For a cold or sinus congestion the pressure point above the inner corner of the eye should be located. It is just below the eyebrow and pressure should be applied until the point feels a little tender. This amount of pressure should be applied for three or four seconds then release. The pressure should be repeated twice more. For nasal congestion the pressure point between the cheekbone and nose is used. Again pressure should be applied three times, for three or four seconds each time. For a cough the point on the hollow of the inner elbow is pressed. The same routine of pressing and releasing should be used again. For more general cold symptoms then the point at the base of the thumb, on the palm side can be pressed. The hollow between the thumb and index finger should be pressed, often using two fingers rather than just one.

Healing touch – acupressure

Insomnia

Place both hands on top of the head. Press down with the middle three fingers for about three seconds then release the pressure. Repeat twice more. Move the fingers round to the base of the skull and put the index and middle fingers in the hollow at the top of the neck. Again press firmly for three seconds and release, repeating this three times. Move the fingers about two finger-widths towards the ears and press and release a further three times. Move the fingers a further two finger-widths and repeat the routine again.

SHIATSU

Shiatsu massage started in China about 2000 years ago. It is based on the eastern belief that energy flows along channels known as meridians. The energy is called Ki in Japan, chi in China and prana in India. Shiatsu clears blockages in these pathways to allow the free flow of energy to maintain health, reduce pain and increase energy. The term shiatsu comes from the Japanese for finger – shi and pressure – atzu.

Shiatsu is useful for headaches, back pain, sleep problems, stress and anxiety, constipation, muscle fatigue, tension, arthritis, stomach upsets, gynaecological problems and general bodily imbalance. It should not be used for fractures, internal problems likely to cause internal bleeding like stomach ulcers or clotting problems. People suffering serious long term illnesses such as cancer or multiple sclerosis should avoid shiatsu. During pregnancy some aspects of shiatsu should also be avoided – pressing on the stomach, the legs below the knees, the areas between the thumb and index finger and the area on the shoulders on either side of the neck.

Shiatsu may help stimulate the energy along a particular meridian to relieve the underlying cause. As part of a holistic therapy exercise, diet and life style changes may also be recommended along with sessions of shiatsu massage.

History and origins

The use of touch and pressure as a form of healing was used by the Chinese at least 5000 years ago. Taoist monks incorporated touch as a form of self-healing into their philosophy. Chinese acupuncture spread to Japan and in the 1700s the principles of acupuncture and massage were combined. Those who practised amma, a form of massage, used their fingers to press and rub painful body parts. It was discovered that if they applied pressure, using their fingers, to acupuncture points then similar effects were felt. The term shiatsu was not itself used until the twentieth century.

Theory and principles

There are certain points on the body which relate to certain internal organs and systems which are

Healing touch – shiatsu

called tsubos. An acupuncturist insets needles into tsubos and a shiatsu therapist applies pressure to these points with the fingers, thumbs, palms and knuckles. They may also use elbows and feet. Shiatsu can be carried out on a self-treatment basis and is principally used to maintain good health rather than treat a long-standing problem.

Shiatsu and other oriental healing techniques are based on the concept of Oneness. Opposing forces, yin and yang, must be kept in balance to achieve Oneness. Yin and yang may be opposites but they also work in harmony. They are not fixed and are constantly changing. Yin is negative and yang positive, although they do not correlate entirely with good and bad in western thought.

According to oriental thinking health problems occur when the balance between these two is disturbed. Prevention is better than cure therefore balance and harmony are important to maintain good health. If however equilibrium is disturbed then healing techniques are necessary to restore balance.

Energy or ki has several layers and centres, as well as channels. Twenty-four pathways form the twelve meridians found on each side of the body. There are two other meridians – the governing and the conception vessels. The governor meridian starts at the jaw, moves over the head and down to the bottom of the spine. The meridian of conception starts at the genital area, runs through the abdomen and chest and ends at the centre of the jaw. The conception meridian in yin and the governing one, yang.

The pathways or meridians pass through the body joining the energy centres, or chakras, and internal body organs. One end of each meridian is under the skin and the other end is on the surface of the skin and feet. Along the meridians are acupressure or acupuncture points – the tsubos. The body has 657 tsubos connected by pathways and channels. These tsubos allow the energy along the pathway to be altered. As they are linked energy can pass from one pathway to another, and as energy is stimulated in one pathway other systems and organs will benefit.

Application and practice
Shiatsu can be self-administered but may also be carried out by a trained practitioner. Clothing should be loose and comfortable. The environment should be warm, quiet and relaxing. The client should lie on a mattress or mat. Small pillows may be required for increased comfort,

Healing touch – shiatsu

especially when lying face down.

Although in general the feeling induced by shiatsu is one of relaxation and wellbeing, occasionally some side effects may be experienced. Coughing, sinus congestion, tiredness, headaches or other aches have been reported. These symptoms may be sparked off by the removal of some blockage and the reestablishment of balance.

Shiatsu is often called shiatsu massage but it is very different from Swedish massage. The trigger points are pressed rather than rubbed, and different procedures require different amounts of pressure. Moderate pressure is applied to the head and lighter pressure to the stomach. Generally firmer pressure is applied to bigger muscles, and body weight rather than muscular strength is important. Pressure should be applied for a short time and both hands should be used. Arms should be extended fully and the movement and pressure should maintain a regular movement and pattern.

The type of shiatsu that is used depends on the type of energy the client has. If energy is low or deficient is is known as kyo, if it is high or excessive then it is known as jitsu. For kyo types the pressure should be gentle, sensitive and held for longer, for jitsu the pressure can be quicker.

A general exercise which can be carried out is known as makko-ho exercises. These are six stretching exercises which stimulate all the meridians in turn and when carried out fully result in increased energy and strength. Before commencing the routine you should be relaxed and comfortable. Some abdominal breathing is often useful to aid relaxation. One exercise is the 'triple heater and heart governor stretch'. Sitting on the ground with feet crossed or together, the right hand should hold the left knee, and the left hand the right knee. Inhale and exhale, during exhalation you should lean forward and down with the top of the body so that the knees are pushed apart. The position should be held for thirty seconds and breathing should be normal then, after inhaling, you should return to the upright position.

If you sit at a desk for many hours there are some simple shiatsu techniques which should help release shoulder and neck tension. With the index finger of one hand locate the midpoint of the opposite shoulder. The point should be slightly behind the main shoulder muscle and should feel tender to pressure, Keep moving your finger until the spot is found. When it is located press firmly for two or three seconds with the

Healing touch – shiatsu

index finger. Release the pressure then repeat pressing twice more. Then find the same spot on the other shoulder and repeat the process. This procedure can also be carried out on another person.

For a headache the sufferer should lie face down on a mat or mattress, with their head facing into the pillow or cushion. Stand with one left on each side of the person at the line of the hips. Bend from the waist and extend your arms straight down to the back of the neck. With the thumb of each hand locate the muscles at the back of the neck where they join the shoulder muscles. There is one on each side of the spine. Place your thumbs on top of the muscle, where the skull meets the neck, one on each side and exert pressure for three or four seconds, then stop. Move your thumbs down about one inch and again exert pressure for three or four seconds and stop. Keep moving the thumbs down in one-inch intervals, pressing and pausing. The last pressure points are at the shoulder line and you should have pressed on at least four points on each side. Then locate the midpoint, just below the base of the skull. Place one thumb on top of the other and press there for three or four seconds, then stop. Repeat this twice more with one or two-second intervals between each pressing.

Along with shiatsu therapy a general wellbeing can be assisted by changes and balance in lifestyle and diet. Diet consists of yin, yang and balanced foods. Balanced food include seeds, nuts, vegetables, fruits and beans. Yin food consists of milk, honey, sugar, alcohol, oil, spices and fruit juices. Drugs are also mostly yin. Yang foods include meat, fish, seafood, eggs, cheese, poultry and salt. Balancing the intake of the different food stuffs is very important. Macrobiotic shiatsu combines macrobiotic diet, breathing, shiatsu and exercise. This comprehensive system helps achieve physical, emotional, mental and environmental balance, as the opposing forces of yin and yang are in harmony.

QIGONG

Qigong – which is pronounced chee-kung – is a form of exercise which combines breathing with ritualised movements which enhance physical, mental and spiritual balance and stimulate the body's natural vital energy force. It is also spelt Chi Kung, Qi Gong, Chi Gong or Chi Gung. Qigong is derived from two words. Qi is the modern Mandarin term for vital energy or breath. Gong can be translated as work or discipline. Thus qigong may be translated as breath work or energy work.

Qigong is useful for asthma and allergies, stomach and digestive disorders such as ulcers and constipation, high blood pressure and other cardiovascular disorders, cancer, weakness or paralysis after stroke as well as other neuromuscular problems such as multiple sclerosis. It has been shown to be beneficial for diabetes, headaches, hepatitis, hormone imbalance, impotence, inflammation, kidney problems, lung and liver disorders and mental health. It is also helpful for stress and anxiety. There are no contraindications to using qigong. A chair and mat are all that are required for carrying out the exercises.

History and origins
Qigong dates from the Chou dynasty in China – 1121 BC – when daoyin was practised. Daoyin was a type of exercise which combined breathing and body movements.

During the sixth century BC Lao-tzu developed his theory of the manipulation of qi or life force by the conscious mind. Buddhism and yoga arrived in China from India during the first century AD and the Chinese adapted yoga to fit with the practice of daoyin and so the technique now known as qigong evolved.

Qigong was very popular in China as it was believed its practice would promote good health, long life and physical fitness. Proponents of martial arts added the power of qi to physical strength but for many qigong was more useful as a treatment for a variety of diseases. Qigong can be used either as a form of self-treatment or a qigong master can channel qi energy through their hands as a form of healing touch.

Healing touch – qigong

During the Cultural Revolution qigong was regarded with disfavour as it was thought to be simply a form of superstition. It was banned during the 1960s but continued to be practised in secret.

Qigong is currently experiencing a revival in interest both in China and beyond. Chinese researchers are keen to study its physiological effects. Currently millions of people practise qigong in public parks in the morning. Its popularity increased after the 1980s when there were two highly-publicised cases which were treated using qigong. A 21-year-old athlete developed lung cancer which was to be treated using orthodox western medicine. He refused this treatment and instead used Guo Lin Gong – a walking form of qigong. He carried out his exercises for fourteen hours a day and, after ten months, his tumour had disappeared. In another case a man was injured during a factory accident. He suffered a fractured skull and spinal injury which resulted in paraplegia. After six months he was treated by a qigong master and immediately he was able to use crutches. Two months later he walked the Great Wall with only a light limp. The Chinese government eventually accepted a scientific basis to qigong and allowed it to be added to the list of accepted treatments available in national hospitals. Although qigong is still relatively unusual in the west, compared to other eastern philosophies and practice, interest in it is growing.

Although scientific research is limited studies have shown that individuals who achieve a relaxed state have a slower heart rate and decreased oxygen consumption and respiration rate. It has also been shown that relaxation aids the immune system. There are also reports of improvement in a number of various conditions or diseases such as cancer, multiple sclerosis, cerebral palsy and paralysis following strokes.

Theory and principles

A vital energy system exists in the body and it is through this that qi – the life force – flows. The paths are called meridians or channels. Along these meridians are energy points which can be treated several ways to alter levels of energy. Treatments which use these meridians include acupuncture, acupressure, heat and qigong. These energy points have been identified and located using electronic instruments because skin resistance at these particular points is lower than for the rest of the skin surface. When energy flows through these channels normally then the body is balanced, healthy and resistant to disease. When there is an imbalance, or blockage, then balance is altered and illness develops.

Qigong can be used to maintain good health and prevent disease, but it can also be used to reestablish balance and health.

Application and practice

Qigong can be practised either indoors or outside. Individual practitioners may include slightly personal elements and variations to some exercises. but the principles are the same. The main emphasis is on the alignment of the body by posture, control and regulation of the breathing, and control of the mind and spirit. All these elements work closely together to control the flow of air in and out of the body to promote a state of relaxation and peacefulness.

Three of the most common qigong routines are the inward training, the strengthening and the relaxation exercise. The movements are stretching and circular and are carried out either lying down, standing or sitting. The movements are very gentle and qigong can be carried out by anyone and does not depend on any particular level of physical fitness. Most people spend about thirty minutes a day doing the exercises, followed by another thirty minutes meditation. After many years serious practice some people become qigong masters, and are believed to be able to emit healing energy from the body and are able to heal others using qi.

An example of qigong exercise involves standing up straight, feet together. Look ahead and breathe naturally. During inhalation stretch the arms above the head as high as possible. When the highest point is reached turn the palms down and let the arms come down slowly to the sides as the breath is exhaled. It is recommended that this routine is repeated eight times a day to reduce stress, but it can also be carried out whenever a feeling of tension is felt.

The relaxation exercises can help relieve stress and tension but when used with other aspects and routines qigong can be a useful exercise to promote personal development.

HERBALISM

History and origins
Herbalism is the study and use of plant material for medicine and health promotion. Herbal remedies can be used to treat disease but also to improve the physical and spiritual quality of life. A fundamental principle is the practice of self-care and treatment by ordinary members of the public but there are also trained herbal practitioners available who are able to treat and advice patients.

The herbs or plants used in treatments are flowering plants, trees, shrubs, mosses, lichen, ferns, algae or funguses. All the plant may be used or only a specific part such as the flowers, bark or root. However, herbal practitioners often also use non plants as healing remedies including animal parts, such as bone, tissue and some organs, insects and animal secretions. Shells, rocks and other minerals are also used. These latter examples are found in ancient Egyptian, Chinese,

European and American manuscripts which are important sources of reference for herbal practitioners. There is no single world-wide system of herbal medicine but they all share similar themes and principles.

Theory and principles

To achieve the optimum level of health and wellbeing. Most herbal systems have specific food, spice and herb taboos and recommendations for certain times or conditions. Herbal medicine emphasises the whole person: mind, body and spirit and stresses the individual. In Chinese herbal medicine individuals with the same medical condition may receive different treatments as each mixture is recommended depending on individual conditions and circumstances.

It is important to find the root cause of the disease and not simply treat the symptoms. The principle of dualism between the healing and life threatening forces if nature is important. In other words the law of nature is the most important factor in any healing. The duality between real and unreal, physical and spiritual, visible and invisible has to be acknowledged. Thus specific time of the day or season of the year may be important factors in the success of any treatment. Emphasis is made of the importance of the cyclical aspect of nature. Thus nature is circular and repeating, although not absolutely predictable. Herbal medicine is open to new plants and uses of plants, as well as to exchange of ideas and knowledge. Professional regulation and accountability is achieved through public reputation and success, rather than through material wealth or image. Herbal practitioners should recognise the limits of their own knowledge and skill. If a case is too complex or beyond the expertise of the herbalist then they will refer to another rather than attempt a course of treatment which might fail.

Lay and professional herbal practitioners
These individuals have a wide knowledge of plants which are useful for health problems but they have not undergone any training in diagnosis and disease management. However, they are likely to be able to evaluate medicinal herbs, their strengths and uses.

Professional herbal practitioners undergo formal training and apprenticeship in plant and medical studies, or plant and healing studies. They are trained to develop extensive knowledge and ability to identify plants, their habitat, preparation, storage, therapeutic indications, dosages, side effects and contraindications. Professional herbal practitioners may come from a family tradition or they may have been selected as having particular potential in this field of healing. These professionals include trained medical herbalists, licensed naturopathic doctors who specialise in botanical medicine, acupuncturists with training in Chinese herbal medicine, Native American herbalists and shamans and Latin American curanderos.

As well as professional and lay herbal practitioners there are those who collect and make up medicines, much like pharmacists do in conventional medicine. Often the professional herbalist does not make up the mixtures themselves but their recommended treatments are made up by others.

Plants
Plants are categorised according to the following classical organisation.
• *Carbohydrates such as sugars and starches and gycosides which are present in plants such as digitalis purpurea leaf and rhubarb root.*
• *Tannins which are present in tea and coffee.*

- *Lipids found in oils and waxes.*
- *Volatile or essential oils such as peppermint of eucalyptus.*
- *Resins.*
- *Natural steroids such as those present in the Mexican yam.*
- *Alkaloids like atropine from Atropa belladonna and morphine from Papaver somniferum.*
- *Peptide hormones.*
- *Enzymes such as bromelain which is found in pineapple.*

There are several conditions and factors which might influence the therapeutic property of a plant of which the herbal practitioner should be aware. These include the habitat or environment of the growing plant such as exposure, location, altitude, rainfall, sun, temperature, wind, soil type and condition, local insects, animals, birds and pests, including human interference from pollution and cultivation. The composition and constituents of active and inert ingredients should also be considered. How and when a particular plant is collected and stored, processed and dispensed as well as the possible presence and effect of any pollutants, pests or disease. The health, status, disease, age of the patient needs to be assessed. Plants also have symbolic or cultural significance which may relate to its efficacy. The possibility of the placebo effect is important and finally the particular social status of the healer is relevant.

Application and practice

There are basic actions of some plants which are associated with specific active constituents. For example respiratory or lung conditions are treated with stimulating expectorants, relaxing expectorants, antitussive, or suppressants, and treatments for infections. Stimulating expectorants include horehound or Marrubium vulgare which is one of the most popular respiratory remedies. Relaxing expectorants or antitussive therapies include cherry laurel or Prunus laurocerasus. Gastrointestinal or digestive conditions including emetics, anti-emetics, laxatives and anti-spasmodics. In large doses ipecacuanha stimulates the stomach to cause vomiting. Ginger or Zingiber officinale can be used to reduce nausea. Senna or Cassia acutiflia or angustifolia is well known for its laxative properties and White Poppy or Papaver somniferum has been used to relieve pain due to its hypnotic and sedative effect.

The nervous system is treated with sedatives,

stimulants, antidepressant and cardiotonics. Sedatives include Valeriana officinalis or valerian. Stimulants such as Kava kava or Piper methysticum have been used, although it also has a depressing effect. Hypericum or St John's wort has been used against depression and hysteria, and Hawthorne or crataegus oxyacanthia is used to treat functional heart problems.

Occasionally plants are found to be inactive or ineffective or may contain poisons. Specific preparation and use can avoid these problems. Often the medicinal ingredient or compound is unidentified or the effect of one part of the plant is different from the effect of the whole plant. Also some plants which were thought to be inert or ineffective have been discovered to be active when more sophisticated testing has been carried out. Many herbal practitioners believe that healing is due to the healing energy of the plants themselves rather than simply the chemical compounds in the plant. Food and medicinal plants often have many effects because of the different compounds. These multiple actions are not a problem since most medicinal plants are not as potent as pharmaceutical drugs.

Some herbs are best used in their fresh form. Others are dried either as whole plants or chopped. In their dried or chopped form they can be prepared as infusions like tea, or heated and simmered as decoctions. Some herbs are prepared as tinctures in alcohol, others require preservation in vinegar extracts and some mix best in glucose syrups or honey. Dried herbs come in tablet, capsule or paste form. Most are taken orally but pessaries, suppositories, creams, enemas, poultices, oils, inhalations, lotions are sometimes more suitable. Herbal medicines work best in slow-acting dosages which are taken consistently and correctly. Since the patient's individual circumstances and symptoms are taken into account often different patients presenting with the same symptoms will be prescribed different herbal remedies.

There is a great need for further research into herbs as both food and medicines. The collection and environment of herbs as well as their pharmacological effects requires more analysis. This scientific knowledge needs to be collected along with the traditional experience of herbalists themselves in order to reach a greater depth of understanding of herbal medicine.

HOMEOPATHY

History and origins

The word homeopathy is derived from the Greek homoeos meaning similar or the same and pathos meaning feeling or suffering.

It was developed by Samuel Hahnemann a German physician and chemist. Between 1790 and 1810 he carried out a series of experiments which showed that substances result in standard signs and symptoms when taken by healthy people. His tests also showed that the medicine whose symptom picture resembled the illness most closely is that one which is most likely to result in a cure for that particular patient.

His theory was that the outward physical signs on illness represented the body's attempt to heal itself. The appropriate remedy therefore would reinforce this natural healing. He invented the term homeopathy to describe his system of using treatments and medicines which imitated the his students, and recorded the symptoms that they provoked. This enabled Hahnemann to build up a list of symptoms caused by medicines.

Today the list of homeopathic treatments includes over 2,000 remedies. Most of the treatments are vegetable in origin: flowers, fruits, bark, leaves, roots. Many can be poisonous in one form; others are quite common well-accepted medicinal plants or herbs. Some of the treatments are mineral and include metals, salts, alkalis and acids. Other remedies are animal in origin and include the poisons of snakes, jellyfish, fish, and other water life; bodily secretions, milk, tissue extracts and also some disease tissue such as abscesses or syphilis.

Theory and principles

Homeopathy is also based on the philosophy of holistic natural healing. Illness is a disturbance of the vital force and results in physical, mental and emotional symptoms which are unique to each person. Therefore it is important that all symptoms are considered before starting any treatment. The patient's lifestyle, emotional wellbeing and feelings are also assessed as well. The method of treatment involves one particular remedy for the whole patient which is based on an

Homeopathy

illness in some way, rather than the more usual method of treating symptoms with a stronger opponent.

Although the early Greek physicians had used similars to treat some treatments Hahnemann developed a systematic philosophy and methodology for diagnosis and treatment. His approach was never accepted by more orthodox medical practitioners and he was ridiculed by many. However, when Hahnemann died he left many important technical manuals and homeopaths were being trained and were practising homeopathy throughout Europe and America.

The homeopathic system is based on treating the sick person rather than a set of rules about illnesses and diseases. In 1790 Hahnemann was carrying out some tests using Peruvian bark or cinchona and ingested some himself. He felt numb, cold and drowsy. He also experienced anxiety and palpitations. The symptoms he experienced were similar to ague or intermittent fever, now known to be a form of malaria, which was one of the diseases that Peruvian bark was prescribed for.

Over the next twenty years he administered medical substances to healthy people, himself or assessment of the totality of symptoms matched with various remedies until the closest match is found. The power and effect of the treatments are related to the response of individual patients. If more than one remedy is administered at a time then it is difficult to know which one has worked.

As the principle of the treatment is based on stimulating a self-healing process rather than correcting an abnormality large or prolonged doses are unnecessary and may also be ineffectual. The smallest possible dose is used and treatment is only repeated if absolutely necessary. The remedy is allowed to complete its action without any interference. The small dose means that it is unlikely that there will be any dangerous side effects. Hahnemann discovered that remedies can still be effective in doses or concentrations that are so small as to be undetectable. Mechanical shaking of the diluted remedies enhances their effect although it is not understood why this should be so. This use of extremely small doses is one of the most controversial aspects of homeopathy as it has never been proven why it works. As a result critics have labelled it no more than placebo medicine.

Homeopathy attempts to identify the order in which symptoms and illnesses appeared, the

Homeopathy

grouping or clustering of any symptoms and the overall relationship to the health and function of the patient. Another backer of homeopathy, Hering, identified four symptom directions.

- *Downwards from the head to the feet.*
- *From inside to the outside.*
- *From vital organs to less vital ones.*
- *From the most recent to the oldest, in reverse order of their appearance.*

Homeopathic medicines are made into remedies by serial dilutions and shaking or succussion in a liquid or solid medium. Basic vegetable materials are crushed and dissolved in 95% grain alcohol, they are then shaken and stored. The same system is used for animal, and any other, products which are soluble in alcohol. Metals and other insoluble remedies are crushed and diluted with lactose, or milk sugar, until they are soluble. The resultant mixture is known as the mother tincture which is then further diluted with alcohol or lactose into 1:10 or X or 1:100 or C. This is then mixed and shaken and is known as 1X or 1C. The process is repeated for 2X or 2C and so on. The most common dilutions for self treatments are 6th, 12th or 30th X or C. Professional treatments use much greater dilutions such as 200C or even 1M.

Application and practice

Patients describe their symptoms and history without interruption. The homeopath encourages the patient to list as many symptoms as possible and a record is made of the patient's list. The homeopath often bases his diagnosis on idiosyncratic features or symptoms which the orthodox practitioner would ignore. The homeopath also determines whether the patient notices any of the following:

• *Any subjective sensations associated with the symptoms such as pain or anger.*
• *Localisation of specific symptoms such as position or side.*
• *If the symptoms relieved or exacerbated by anything such as weather, time of day or diet.*
• *If any symptoms appear at the same time or in sequence.*

The homeopath will also physically examine the patient and carry out any necessary laboratory tests to confirm diagnosis.

As the case history is taken symptoms are assessed in terms of importance depending on how the patient describes them. The vast range of possible remedies available means that the homeopath requires to use the repertory, which is an index of symptoms and remedies which have proved effective. By identifying remedies appropriate to the main symptoms the total search is narrowed down. The remedies found in the repertory are only suggestions, and the symptoms and remedies need to be assessed carefully before the final selection is made.

Many of the dilute remedies are inactivated by sunlight and therefore require to be stored in dark, dry places. Patients are not allowed to put anything in their mouths for at least 30 minutes before and after each dose. Coffee can reverse the effects of the remedy, and it is recommended that it is avoided throughout the period of the treatment. The use of other herbal medicines and exposure to mothballs, and other highly aromatic substances, should be avoided. Unless absolutely necessary, as in the case of severely ill patients, other conventional drugs should also be stopped. Treatments such as chiropractic and acupuncture should not be commenced at the same time as homeopathy, however if they are already being used then treatment should continue.

Treatment
Remedies are available in the form of tablets of sucrose or lactose and are taken dry on the tongue or dissolved in water. They are also available in liquid form. If taken in the tablet form then they should be sucked or allowed to dissolve on the tongue rather than being swallowed. The more acute the condition is then the lower the dilution so they can be repeated as often as necessary. Higher dilutions are used by professionals for chronic or long-term conditions. Use of higher dilutions should be carefully administered and they should not be taken while their action is still in progress. The dosage prescribed by the homeopath refers to the number and frequency of repetitions which is recommended for each individual patient. The remedy is stopped once any reaction is seen and repeated only when the reaction stops.

There are very few contraindications to homeopathy. Even patients with severe chronic diseases or drug dependency can be offered some help. Prednisolone – which is a commonly prescribed steroid taken to relieve long term inflammatory conditions – does diminish the effect of homeopathic remedies. Nevertheless this does not mean that homeopathic remedies cannot be taken at the same time, the dosage schedule can be adjusted to compensate. Remedies are economic, safe, easy to use and have very few serious side effects. The reactions may seem unnoticeable at first, they are long-lasting and effective. However, homeopathy is a difficult practice and even a skilled homeopath may need to try several remedies before seeing any reaction. Since the remedies are so delicate and easily inactivated then careful precautions must be observed.

Homeopathy is most appropriate for functional conditions, such as headaches, menstrual complaints or fatigue, where there is little or no tissue damage. Conditions where no other conventional treatment is available. For example multiple sclerosis, AIDS, viral illnesses and traumatic injuries. Conditions which necessitate the long-term use of conventional drugs such as allergies, arthritis and digestive problems. Conditions where elective surgery is possible but not urgent. For example uterine fibroids, gallstones and haemorrhoids. conditions which for some reason have not been cured by conventional treatments.

Homeopathy is not useful in treating long-term diseases such as liver cirrhosis or heart disease; or for those patients who require anti convulsants, steroids and psychotropic drugs. Homeopathy is also not an alternative to surgery or repair of fractures.

Some common homeopathic remedies
Aconite (also known as monkshood, wolfsbane, friar's cap, blue rocket and old wife's hood) – used for fevers; illnesses and infections of sudden onset which have associated pain; colds, influenza and other respiratory tract infections; eye problems; urine infections; arthritis, hepatitis; angina and heart failure; nervous conditions including epilepsy; menopausal conditions and some emotional conditions such as panic attacks, anxiety and fear.

Allium cepa or onion – used in conditions associated with tears and nasal and throat irritations including allergies, hayfever, rhinitis and colds. Also useful for pain associated with headaches, toothache and earache, particularly in children.

Aloe – is used for headaches; prostrate problems, uterine prolapses; haemorrhoids and piles; constipation and over indulgence in alcohol.

Homeopathy

Apis mellifica or Honey Bee – used for conditions which have severe stinging pains such as inflammations, redness, swelling and itching of the skin. Also useful in treating insect stings and bites, nettle rash, blisters, prickly heat and allergic reactions particularly those associated with heat. Can also help urinary infections and renal problems; angina associated with fluid retention; inflamed joints including rheumatoid arthritis, and gallstones.

Arnica *(also known as Leopard's bane, mountain tobacco)* – used as a first aid remedy for injuries involving bleeding, swelling, sprains, bruising and pain. It is also thought to help healing and can be useful after surgery and trauma. It can help cystitis and urine retention after injury, gout and other rheumatic problems such as arthritis, muscles pain and inflammation. Can be used for angina; skin conditions such as eczema and boils; halitosis or bad breath; recovery from strokes; and anxiety and phobias about open spaces and being touched. It can help whooping cough and bed wetting in children.

Belladonna *(also known as deadly nightshade, devil's herb, devil's cherries, black cherries,* *dwayberry)* – is used for acute conditions which occur suddenly and involve fever. The symptoms include headache, red flushed skin, thumping heart and cold hands. Diseases include infectious ones such as influenza; tonsillitis and sore throats; coughs; bronchitis; pleurisy; chicken pox; measles; mumps; skin infections; swollen glands; whooping cough and pneumonia. Neuralgia; earache; sinusitis; conjunctivitis and glaucoma; migraines and headaches; toothache; boils and kidney infections can all be treated with belladonna. It is also helpful in cases of hepatitis with pain in the upper stomach; skin abscesses; infective arthritis; fear or phobia of dogs; manic depression; heavy periods and labour pains; painful breasts during breast feeding and fever and teething in children.

Bryonia *(also known as wild hops, English mandrake, wild vine, lady's seal, tetterbury)* – used for inflammation in arthritic and rheumatic disorders; pleurisy, bronchitis and other respiratory conditions; vomiting, nausea, constipation and other digestive problems; breast inflammation during breast feeding; colic in babies; labyrinthitis, migraine and headaches.

Calcarea carbonica or calcium carbonate – used for bone and teeth disorders including osteoarthritis; headaches and eye problems; ear infections; tuberculosis, coughs and colds; hormonal problems such as premenstrual syndrome or heavy periods; eczema and skin conditions; gallstones, kidney and bladder stones and anxiety and depression.

Cantharis or Spanish Fly – used for conditions associated with stinging pain. Urine retention or kidney stones; digestive problems such as diarrhoea, bloating and irritable bowel; insect bites and stings; sunburn; prickly heat and some anxiety or emotional conditions which involve irritable or violent behaviour.

Chamomilla *(also known as chamomil, anthemis nobilis)* -- is used for teething; colic and night crying in children; menstrual problems such as heavy periods; toothache; digestive problems and cystitis.

Cinchona officinalis *(known as Peruvian bark, cinchona succiruba, chincona officinalis, china, Jesuit's bark)* – is used for mental and physical conditions associated with chronic debilitating illness and loss of body fluids. These include influenza type illnesses associated with symptoms of sweating, chills, fever, weakness and headache. It is also useful for muscle spasm due to tiredness or neuralgia; digestive problems; heavy periods; apathy and loss of concentration and depression.

Digitalis *(known as foxglove, digitalis purpurea, fairy thimbles, fairy caps, dead men's bells, witches' gloves, virgins's gloves and folk's gloves)* – is used for heart disorders with a faint or irregular beat. There may also be other symptoms associated with right-sided heart failure such as kidney problems and fluid retention.

Ferrum metallicum or iron – used for anaemia and circulation problems which feature tiredness, malaise, pallor and exhaustion. Is useful for anaemia in pregnancy. Can also help headaches, migraines and depression.

Graphite – helps skin conditions such as eczema, psoriasis, acne, dry skin and blisters. It can also help ear infections, thickened and cracked nails and cold sores. Stomach and duodenal ulcers; cramps; menstrual problems and lumbago can also be helped with graphite, as can some depressive symptoms.

Hellebore (known as black hellebore, helleborus, Christmas rose, Christmas herb, melampode) – is used for severe headaches with stabbing pains. Epilepsy may also be connected to the headaches. Kidney disease and oedema can also be treated with hellebore.

Hyoscyamus *(also known as henbane, hyoscyamus niger, henbell, hogbean)* – used to treat paranoia, jealousy, and unreasonable or aggressive behaviour. Muscular spasms and crampy pains and disorders of the digestive or urinary systems may be treated with henbane. Alcoholism with hiccups and vomiting may also respond to its use.

Iodume or iodine – used to treat hyperthyroidism, pancreatic disorders and disorders of the spleen. Coughs, laryngitis and throat problems; breathlessness and anxiety can be treated with iodine.

Ledum *(known as Marsh tea, wild rosemary, ledum palustre)* – is used as a first aid remedy for insect stings, animal bites, cuts and bruises. Can also be used for rheumatic pains and cataracts experienced by those suffering from gout.

Lycopodium (or *Club moss, lycopodium clavatum, wolf's claw, vegetable sulphur, stag-horn's moss, running pine*) – used to treat digestive and kidney conditions including indigestion, heartburn, sickness, nausea, wind, bloatedness and constipation. Cystitis and urine retention; haemorrhoids; right-sided problems and nettle rash, psoriasis, ME-type problems, headaches, coughs and ear problems; gout and arthritis; stress, anxiety and apprehension associated with insecurity and fear; insomnia and sleep problems can be helped with lycopodium.

Magnesia muriaticum or magnesium chloride – used to treat neuralgia, cramp and spasm; colicky pains such as gallstones, diverticulitis, irritable bowel syndrome or ulcerative colitis.

Mercurius solubis or mercury – used for problems associated with excretions and sweating. Inflammation of the gums; eye infections and conjunctivitis; bad breath; mouth ulcers; nappy rash; infected throats and colds; colicky pains; Parkinson's disease and allergic reactions such as runny nose and skin problems can be treated with mercury.

Nitric acidium or nitric acid – used to treat sharp, stabbing pains associated with piles or haemorrhoids, constipation, swollen saliva glands, skin ulcers, sore throat and tonsillitis. Pneumonia, kidney stones and depression associated with rages and irritable behaviour can also be treated with nitric acid.

Nux vomica *(known as poison nut, strychnos nux vomica, Quaker buttons)* – can be used to treat digestive problems such as indigestion, nausea, vomiting, diarrhoea, constipation, cramps and colic. Other abdominal pains such as kidney or gallstones respond to nux vomica as well as overeating, too much alcohol, coffee and rich food. Migraines and other headaches, hayfever, allergic rhinitis, colds and sore throats also respond to nux vomica. Other conditions which may be helped include: cystitis; acne; back pain especially following labour; heavy periods; epilepsy; impotence; stroke; mania or overwork and sleep problems in babies.

Opium *(known as opium poppy, papaver somniferum, mawseed)* – helps symptoms of mental shock associated with fright. Alcoholism with DTs, hallucinations, and unconsciousness associates with drinking binges; respiratory problems; urine retention; paralysis after stroke and epilepsy where the convulsion is stimulated by heat can be helped with opium.

Phosphorus – helps conditions of acute anxiety caused by stress and worry which are accompanied by exhaustion, insomnia and indigestion. Gastric symptoms which can be helped include nausea, vomiting, indigestion, diarrhoea and halitosis. Minor wounds and bleeding; respiratory symptoms; poor circulation; giddiness or labyrinthitis; cataracts and glaucoma; morning sickness and night crying or sleep problems in babies can be treated with phosphorus.

Rhus toxicodendron *(known as American poison ivy, poison oak, poison vine)* – treats muscle and joint inflammation; eczema and other skin problems; fever symptoms associated with viral infections; back pain; Parkinson's disease; menstrual problems; right-sided strokes and depression and anxiety.

Sanguinaria *(also known as blood root, sanguinaria canadensis, red puccoon, sweet slumber, snakebit, coon root, Indian plant)* – is used to treat chest and respiratory problems such as bronchitis, pneumonia, asthma, rhinitis, whooping cough, colds, flue, hayfever, migraine and other headaches. Acne; hot flushes and heavy periods can also be helped by sanguinaria.

Sepia or **ink of the cuttlefish** – can be used to treat premenstrual syndrome, bleeding and other menstrual problems associated with the menopause. Also used in pregnancy for early morning sickness; other problems associated with hormonal imbalance; gastric problems including nausea, cramps, wind and pain; cystitis and bladder pain; foot problems such as veruccas; nettle rash; back pain; and depression where the person withdraws and wants to be left alone.

Valerian officinalis *(known also as great wild valerian, all-heal, setwell, capon's tail)* – is used for agitation, restlessness and anxiety associated with muscle spasms, hysteria, headache and pains. Sleep problems and diarrhoea may also be helped.

These are only a sample of the type and range of

treatments and remedies available and for more detailed information and advice a specialist book or practitioner should be consulted.

The future of homeopathy

Homeopathic treatment is increasing throughout Europe, Latin America and Asia. Even in Britain 42% of physicians refer patients to homeopaths. As the cost of conventional allopathic medicine increases more and more developing countries are using it as a cheaper alternative.

LIGHT THERAPY

Light, or heliotherapy, is the treatment of disease by sunlight. Phototherapy uses artificial light to relieve symptoms. Biological processes repeat themselves at regular intervals and are controlled by internal and external environmental factors. It is the circadian rhythms which have periods matching the solar day which are most important. Thus blood pressure, temperature, hormone production and digestive processes are different at various times of the day.

Light therapy is useful in the treatment of hair loss, impotence, dermatitis and other skin conditions such as eczema, psoriasis, scleroderma and vitiligo, rheumatoid arthritis and jet lag. Depression, sleep problems, irritability, seasonal affective disorder or SAD, and alcohol abuse may also be helped by light therapy.

The dangers of over-exposure to light, especially sunlight or sun lamps, cannot be over-emphasised. It can cause serious damage to the skin and may increase the risk of skin cancer in later life. Therefore the length of any treatment with sun lamps or natural sunlight should be carefully controlled, sunscreens should be applied and sunglasses worn to protect the eyes.

History and origins

Awareness of the power of the sun was important to many early societies. Some cultures worshipped the sun as the most powerful and creative force. The Aztecs, Mayans and Incas of South and Central America practised sun worship and sacrifice. The Egyptians, Greeks and Romans worshipped many gods although the sun god was one of the most important and powerful.

Many calendar customs and rituals of ancient, and our own, cultures related to solar cycles – the winter and summer solstices being the most important.

Chinese doctors recognised that the human body also had its own daily, monthly and yearly cycles. Hippocrates used the ritual of sun baths, or heliotherapy, to help heal wounds and weakened muscles. Solariums were built by Romans on the top of their houses so they could enjoy sunbathing. By the eighteenth century French doctors treated leg ulcers and wounds using

Light therapy

sunlight.

Theory and principles

The first observations about circadian rhythms were noted during experiments on the heliotrope flower which demonstrated the same pattern of opening and turning during a 24-hour cycle even when it was not exposed to sunlight. Thus it was realised that every plant and animal has its own circadian rhythm which is not governed by solar influences. Animals living in controlled environments with constant temperature, illuminations and other variations continue to show an approximate 24-hour cycle of activity and rest. When a light-dark cycle was imposed some animals do demonstrate some tendency to adapt to the imposed cycle but their own internal clock was still relevant. It is now recognised that there is a link between the internal daily clock and an external light-dark cycle. The pineal gland, located in the brain, responds to information about light received from the eyes and the rest of the body. The pineal gland secretes a high amount of melatonin during darkness, and very little during daylight hours, and it is thought that melatonin serves as the body's darkness indicator and lowers temperature and switches off other bodily functions during these hours.

Application and practice
Sunlight contains the full range of light necessary to maintain life but most artificial light lacks some of the spectrum. Most people work in environments illuminated by fluorescent lights rather than natural light, and this artificial light affects health, productivity and emotional well-being.

Bright light therapy uses broad-spectrum white light, and for people suffering from SAD exposure for 30 minutes first thing in the morning is helpful. The exposure time depends on the strength of the light and individual requirements. The brightness of the light should be between 2,500 and 10,000 lux. A lux being the equivalent to the amount of brightness given off by a candle – one candle equals one lux.

Sunlight produces vitamin D in the skin. Vitamin D is necessary for strong bones and teeth and, although supplements are available, regular exposure to daylight either by walking or playing will enhance the body's natural production of this vitamin. Vitamin D helps increase calcium absorption which strengthens bones. Increasing the strength of bones is important for children

Light therapy

and older people. For older people the increased risk of fractures, especially the hip, due to osteoporosis is a particular danger.

For those suffering skin disorders treatment by sunlight is often helpful. Exposure should be built up, and midday should be avoided as the damage from ultraviolet rays outweighs any possible benefits. If natural sunlight is in short supply – for example in a northern climate – then use of an artificial full-spectrum light source is a good alternative. It is important not to use a sunlamp as the dangers from overexposure cannot be emphasised enough. A full-spectrum light source is not the same as an ultraviolet sunlamp.

Jet lag can also be assisted by altering the circadian rhythm. Avoid morning sunlight on the day of departure, during the flight and the day of your arrival by shielding your eyes as much as possible wearing very dark sunglasses or goggles. At the same time get as much exposure to afternoon sunlight as possible. This can help adjust your body clock by as much as three hours per day.

MAGNETIC THERAPY

Magnetic therapy uses magnetism to promote healing and well-being. Magnets do not cure conditions, but stimulate the body's own natural healing processes.

It is useful in cases of sprains, strains, bruises, fractures, chronic pain, wounds, burns, headaches, infections, oedema, rheumatic disease and circulation problems. Those suffering from insomnia and other sleep disorders, as well as stress, may also benefit from magnetic therapy.

MAGNETIC THERAPY SHOULD NOT BE USED DURING PREGNANCY.

Ordinary bar or horse shoe magnets are not therapeutic magnets. Those magnets which are used by therapists may be hard and inflexible, but others can be more flexible and flat. The magnetic element may be ceramic, neodynmium or plastiform, and they have a permanent magnetic charge. Flexible magnets of various sizes are available to suit different purposes and body parts. Some come in the form of bracelets, necklaces, mattress pads, pillows and shoe insoles.

History and origins

The Greeks, Chinese, Egyptians and Indians recognised the healing power of magnetism. The natural ability of the iron ore, or lodestone, for iron was intriguing for people and many thought these lodestones had magical properties. They often wore small amulets of lodestone around their necks or wrists. Galen, the Greek physician, discovered that pain could be relieved by placing pieces of natural magnet, or lodestone, on various parts of the body.

With the discovery that magnets would naturally turn to the north the compass was invented, and by the end of the eighteenth century Franz Mesmer, an Austrian doctor, used magnets to cure disease. Mesmer eventually abandoned this technique but replaced it with mesmerism – a hypnotic technique – to restore magnetic fluid to diseased people. Mesmer believed that disease was caused by an imbalance of magnetic fluid which was contained in the body. Although Mesmer was again discredited his techniques laid the ground for later hypnotic techniques, and his earlier interest in the use of magnets helped develop

Magnetic therapy

further studies in this area.

Russian and Japanese doctors used magnets to relieve pain from wounds during World War II. Russian doctors have also used magnets to treat heart and nerve disorders.

Theory and principles

The magnets stimulate the body's own natural healing processes. The body's system is controlled by ionic currents and electromagnetic fields. Static magnetic fields can be produced by magnets, and these magnetic fields can penetrate and affect the function of the nervous system, internal organs and cells. A negative magnetic field can increase metabolic rate, which then stimulates the flow of blood and oxygen to damaged cells. By increasing oxygenation and reducing acidity magnetic stimulation restores the body to a naturally alkaline well-oxygenated environment which is not a bacteria-friendly environment thus reducing the chance of infection.

All magnets have a negative and a positive pole. The point, or part, of the pole which points to the north is the negative pole. It is believed that the negative pole has a calming effect and restores normal metabolism, whereas the positive pole increases stress, interferes with metabolism and induces illness.

Application and practice

One or more magnets are placed on the body above the various organs, on points of the head, over lymph nodes and above bruises and other injuries. Treatment can be as quick as a couple of hours or overnight, and the full course may take several days or weeks. In some conditions magnets should be applied at various times in the day. Negatively charged mattress pads or blankets can also be used for long-term treatments.

A negative magnetic field applied to the top of the head relaxes and promotes sleep. It is thought that negative energy stimulates melatonin production which also reduces stress.

It is best not to try magnetic therapy without advice from a trained practitioner. They can give instructions about the the best methods of application for particular problems. Magnetic therapy is quite safe but there are some guidelines which should be observed. The positive magnetic pole should not be used without professional advice as it induces stress and illness. A magnetic blanket or bed should not be used for more than 10 hours a day. After eating a period of one and a half hours should elapse before using magnetic

Magnetic therapy

therapy in order not to interfere with the digestion of food. Magnetic therapy should not be used on the abdomen during pregnancy.

MEDITATION

There are several types and techniques of meditation but they all serve to focus the conscious mind inwardly in order to connect with our inner being. Transcendental meditation is an important aspect of ayurvedic medicine, but meditation can be used along with t'ai chi, yoga, aromatherapy and other breathing exercise regimes and is associated with a number of religion,s notably Buddhism.

Meditation is particularly useful for high blood pressure and other cardiac and cardiovascular problems, sleep disorders, headaches and chronic pain. Those suffering from stress and anxiety, depression, lack of mental awareness, low self-esteem and general debility may also benefit from meditation therapy.

Those who are experienced meditators can often meditate in any environment and are able to ignore external stimuli, but for those starting to learn meditation techniques a quiet, comfortable and safe environment is best. Meditation can be done either sitting on the floor, on a chair or lying down. With more experience it is possible to meditate outside in the fresh air. With the repetition of sounds, chants or prayers people can free their minds. A similar process was often used before battle by Native Americans

History and origins
Meditation has been associated with all forms of religious worship. Quiet contemplation allowed a focusing of the mind and communication with the spirit. In the east meditation is practised by ordinary people not only as part of their religious worship but as part of their daily routine. In the west meditation became popular through the introduction of transcendental meditation by Maharishi Mahesh Yogi.

Theory and principles
According to ayurvedic philosophy there should be a balanced connection between the conscious mind and the unconscious spirit, and that good physical health is dependent on the state of this relationship. Scientific studies have shown that meditation can reduce stress and blood pressure. The whole body metabolism and brain activity

take on a new pattern of rest and balance. It has been shown that during a state of relaxation the metabolic activity achieved is lower than that experienced during sleep. Some studies have demonstrated that respiration can be suspended without any oxygen deprivation. Maharishsi's theory was that there were four states of human consciousness – waking, sleeping, dreaming and transcendental.

Application and practice
One form of meditation starts with the body and then progresses to the mind. The other relates only to the mind with no reference to the body. An example of the former is hatha yoga where the body is controlled by practising postures and exercises and then progresses to a focusing of the conscious mind by meditation. The most well-known meditation posture is the lotus position but there are other ones which are equally suitable. The important features are a straight back and a steady, non-changing position either on the floor or on a chair. It is also recommended that mediation is done alone with no other external distractions which might disturb concentration. Once the position is achieved then the eyes should be shut and the breathing done

rhythmically, through the nose. The mind should then be concentrated on a single object, word or image although the ultimate object is not to think about anything. A meditative state is not about focusing and thinking but about reaching a different state of consciousness.

Another approach to meditation is to physically relax the body rather than attempt to control it. In this method the technique is to concentrate on relaxing each part of the body in turn. This method can be carried out lying down as opposed to the yoga sitting position. Sometimes it is easiest to tense the muscles first and then relax them. Repeating a phrase such as "I am warm, I am relaxed" can also be helpful. Often the mantra may just be a single word and the most familiar is the Sanskrit term oom.

A further version of the mantra technique is the western Relaxation Response. A word can be selected which is repeated at each exhalation while sitting in a relaxed, comfortable position. Alternatively thinking about a single image, such as a shape, can be used to help clear the mind of other distractions. Some people find visualising a peaceful and safe environment, such as a warm, sunny beach, helpful. One of the simplest methods of mental focusing is to concentrate on establishing a steady rhythmic breathing pattern. Respiration rate should not be changed consciously instead the natural rate should be maintained. Breathing should be done through the nostrils and not the mouth, and as the mediation progresses the breathing should naturally become slower and more relaxed.

These approaches are all concentrative meditation. A different system is known as mindfulness meditation. This allows the mind to wander freely during meditation but each thought, image or idea should be noted. No subjective analysis should be made about the ideas or feelings.

Meditation can be learnt with practice and instruction can be found in books and tapes. Transcendental Meditation requires teaching by a qualified instructor.

NATUROPATHY

Naturopathy, or natural medicine, is a system of health care which stresses the prevention of disease and the use of natural treatments to stimulate the body's own healing powers. It is as much a way of life as a system of health care. Those who believe in naturopathy use many different forms of alternative therapies such as acupuncture, hydrotherapy, homeopathy and diet. They are non-invasive but if the condition is life-threatening or a serious injury then more orthodox methods are necessary.

Health is seen by naturopaths as being more than the absence of disease but the dynamic state which enables a person to function despite external or internal stresses.

It is useful for all diseases and conditions which do not require immediate orthodox surgical or medical therapy. It is most useful in chronic or long term conditions such as arthritis and chronic pain. Naturopathic medicine is also helpful for those suffering from tension, stress, depression, sleep problems and substance addiction.

History and origins

Naturopathic medicine can trace its origins back to the theories of Greek physicians such as Hippocrates. Hippocrates believed that diseases had natural physical causes and that rational cures could be found in nature. Although this form of medical belief had ancient origins, the form of medicine now classified as naturopathy did not originate until the nineteenth century. The word naturopathy was used by Dr John Scheel, a German doctor, who practised medicine in New York towards the end of the nineteenth century. He referred to a system of healing which worked on the whole person and used natural methods. Another important influence on the development of naturopathic medicine was Father Sebastian Kneipp who popularised hydrotherapy in Europe. By the twentieth century Benedict Lust, another German, increased the range of treatments to include diet, exercise, herbs, manipulation and homeopathy as well as Kneipp's Germanic tradition of hydrotherapy. Lust qualified as an osteopath in 1898 and opened a 'Health Food

Naturopathy

Store' which sold organically-grown produce and was the first such outlet to use the term 'health food'. By 1902 Lust began using the term naturopathy and he founded the American School of Naturopathy and the Naturopathic Society of America. In 1919 this became the American Naturopathic Association.

One of the earliest forms of naturopathic therapy was the German hydrotherapy movement. They maintained that the use of hot and cold water was essential for health and the treatment of disease. Water treatments and spas have a long history of popularity dating from Roman times into the early-modern period. During the nineteenth century water sanitariums or spas became very popular.

Natural living, a vegetarian diet, and the use of air and light are all important aspects of the Nature Cure movement. It was founded in Austria by Dr Arnold Rickli in 1848 who advocated a vegetarian diet. Dr Henry Lahman started a Nature Cure institute near Dresden in Germany and he was the first to develop appliances to administer electric light treatment.

The Hygienic System incorporated vegetarianism, hydrotherapy and nature cure movements. It also started in the nineteenth century and was founded by Sylvester Graham in 1830. John Tilden developed a theory of auto-intoxication and toxaemia which stated that many problems were caused by constipation and the retention of waste matter. Homeopathy, developed by Samuel Hahnemann, was also part of the naturopathic school of medical thought. His theory was that disease could be treated by the law of similars or that like treated like. He also believed that the effect of a medicine was increased by smaller, rather than larger, doses. Manipulation, such as osteopathy, was another aspect of naturopathy. It emphasises that the structural integrity of the body is important in maintaining health.

Theory and principles
Benedict Lust believed that the best lifestyle should exclude harmful habits such as smoking and alcohol, eating meat, drinking tea and coffee, overeating and lack of sleep. A better daily lifestyle emphasised a good selection of diet, physical exercise, breathing exercises and a healthy positive attitude. He believed that nature can help the body overcome disease better by intrinsic, natural means rather than by the use of artificial drugs. During the early decades of the twentieth century

naturopathic medicine flourished and both orthodox and naturopathic medicine were used interchangeably. As chemically-produced medicine and drugs developed orthodox allopathic physicians prescribed them rather than use the older herbal-based formulas. As technology advanced surgical methods became increasingly sophisticated and naturopathy, and other forms of alternative medicine, became increasingly marginalised and excluded by the powerful coalition of orthodox medicine and national governments.

However, by the late twentieth century society started to review its attitudes towards orthodox medicine and alternative systems of health care. There has been an increased awareness that chemical medicines and technologically-based surgery may not always provide the best cures or answers and instead many people are actively seeking other forms of treatments.

With the discovery of the importance of vitamins and minerals in maintaining a healthy body some of the theories of naturopathic therapies have now been understood on a more scientific basis. As scientists identified the link between enzymes and nutrients then the importance of organic whole foods became more acceptable. Later scientific research by Rachel Carson has demonstrated that toxic load can be measured and provide objective evidence.

As has already been pointed out naturopathy is not one form of treatment but combines many systems of healing. Some practitioners specialise in a preferred method of treatment, while others offer a variety and combination of therapies. As restoration of normal function is the goal then a selection of therapies may be tried in order that the body's own healing processes are supported. There is a wide range of naturopathic practitioners, from those who believe in a strict cure by natural diet, detoxification and lifestyle changes to those who use botanical or herbal remedies rather than chemically manufactured drugs. However, there are some fundamental beliefs which run through all forms of naturopathic medicine. One is that prevention is better than cure. Two, that although the practitioner can advise the sufferer about lifestyle the person must take an active part in achieving a state of wellbeing and maintaining it themselves. Naturopathic medicine also treats the whole person not just the symptoms, therefore all aspects of the individual's life are considered when advice is given or treatments prescribed.

Naturopathy

The most important element is that nature is the greatest healer and, because the treatments are based on natural elements, the side effects are less traumatic.

Application and practice

Naturopathic medicine often involves a change in attitude towards ill health and its cure. Instead of turning immediately to analgesia for pain it may be better to use massage, exercise, a sleep or herbal remedies. Part of the approach is to identify the cause of the ill health or symptom and attempt to reduce or remove it, rather than always treating the symptoms themselves. Symptoms which are related to particular diseases are not only caused by the bacteria, or other agent, but by the body's reaction to the agent. If symptoms are related to stress, or a specific pattern of behaviour, then naturopaths recommend stress reducing strategies. It is best not to wait for the symptoms to increase but to eliminate them completely or start a procedure at the earliest sign. The eventual ideal is to incorporate a stress reducing ritual into a daily routine. This may take the form of a bath, a walk, a massage or a herbal tea.

The most effective diagnosis and treatment

approach is to consider the whole person. It is often referred to as holistic medicine. Jan Christian Smuts coined the term holism to describe a system where the total was greater than the sum of its parts. In other words the mental, emotional and spiritual wellbeing are all important, as are family life, lifestyle, diet and environment. It is important to assess individual circumstances and needs to ensure effective treatment. Patient education and responsibility are also vital to the success of any therapy and, therefore, some alteration in lifestyle may be necessary to maintain wellbeing.

Examples of the naturopathic approach to disease can be seen in the conditions of migraines and high blood pressure. For migraine headache the allopathic approach would be to use drugs to relieve the symptoms. The naturopathic approach might suggest that the headaches may be due to food allergies and that there is an abnormal metabolic reaction to the nutritional imbalance which causes the symptoms. The recommended treatment would be identification and avoidance of the allergic foods. Magnesium supplements can be useful, as migraine sufferers often have generally lowered magnesium levels which are reduced even more during an attack. By decreasing animal fats a normal prostaglandin balance is established, which can be enhanced with essential fatty acids by taking fish oil supplements.

Those suffering from high blood pressure can be treated with the following lifestyle changes. Excessive intake of salt, as well as an inadequate intake of potassium, can contribute to hypertension. Low calcium, magnesium, essential fatty acids and vitamin C may also cause high blood pressure, as well as high sugar, caffeine and alcohol consumption. Smoking, stress and a sedentary lifestyle with little exercise may also lead to the development of high blood pressure. All the above can be addressed either by reducing intake, taking supplements or taking increased exercise. There are also herbal medicines which can lower blood pressure safely which can be used until changes in lifestyle can take effect.

In another example for those who experience irritable bowel syndrome (IBS) naturopathic advice would include information about diet. Sugar, coffee, refined foods and those with chemical additives should be avoided as much as possible as they disrupt the body's ability to absorb minerals and vitamins. Vitamin B is particularly important for IBS and sources rich in vitamin B are brown rice, wholewheat bread, pork, eggs, vegetables, soya beans, liver and brewer's yeast. Often IBS is associated with food intolerance. Commonly these are dairy products, wheat, citrus fruits, yeasts, sugar, alcohol, coffee, chocolate and shellfish. Naturopathic practitioners will recommend an exclusion diet where these foods are excluded for two weeks, after the two weeks they are reintroduced one at a time. Often there is a marked reaction to one particular food which can be avoided in the future. Although diet is the preferred form of therapy naturopathic practitioners may suggest vitamin and mineral supplements. Lactobacillus Acidopholus can also be helpful. This bacteria is crucial for digesting food and some individuals may be deficient in it, especially if there has been long term use of antibiotics.

For those suffering from osteoarthritis naturopathic treatment again concentrates on diet. Fat is often associated with joint inflammation. Animal fat found in red meat and dairy products, heated oils and fats, and hardened (hydrogenated) oils found in margarine should be avoided. Other oils help reduce inflammation. These are fish oils or EPAs and nut oils or GPAs. Cooking oils such as soya, peanut and safflower are also anti-inflammatory. Avoidance of foods such as tomatoes, aubergines, peppers, potatoes and tobacco is also recommended. Anti-oxidants may help reduce inflammation. These include vitamins A, C and E and the minerals zinc and selenium. Foods rich in vitamin A are fish liver, carrots, green and yellow vegetables and yellow fruit. Citrus fruits, berries, green, leafy vegetables, tomatoes and cauliflower are high in vitamin C. Wheatgerm, soya beans, broccoli, Brussels sprouts, nuts and cereals are high in vitamin E. Zinc is found in wheatgerm, brewer's yeast, pumpkin seeds and mustard seeds; and selenium is found in bran, tuna, onions, tomatoes, broccoli and wheatgerm. Vitamin P or quercitin is also useful. It works with vitamin C and also helps reduce joint destruction. It is found in the white skin and segment parts of citrus fruits, buckwheat, apricots and cherries. However, high acid foods such as citrus fruits, berries, rhubarb can also increase joint problems therefore these foods should be taken with care. Coffee, alcohol, tea, sugar, chocolate and smoking can interfere with the absorption of the essential minerals and vitamins from the food. Some vitamin supplements may be necessary. Antioxidant Formula is useful, as are Cod Liver Oil capsules.

Calcium and magnesium supplement is often recommended. Gentle exercise is also recommended during periods of remission from pain. Swimming is a particularly good choice. It can help maintain the flexibility and mobility of the joints and prevent muscle wasting. Other lifestyle changes recommended by naturopathic practitioners include dieting if overweight and stopping smoking.

With increased scientific research naturopathic medicine may be increasingly accepted. Even allopathic medicine now includes such lifestyle changes as described above in their recommendations for health care. There has been a change in medical attitudes and what was once seen as faddish and eccentric is now seen as being quite effective and can be incorporated into orthodox medical practice.

OSTEOPATHY

Osteopathy emphasises that maintaining physical and mental well-being is dependent on the structural integrity of the body mechanism. Diagnosis and therapy is based on using the close relationship between anatomy and physiology. Healing is based on restoring structural and mechanical normality or balance.

History and origins

The American School of Osteopathy was founded in 1892, although some of the principles of the philosophy and practice had been developed some years earlier by Andrew Taylor Still. Still practised as an orthodox allopathic physician and surgeon, but the loss of three of his children to meningitis in 1864 caused him to reject the use of drugs and reassess his use and application of allopathic medicine. He developed his osteopathic ideas despite much opposition and in 1892 he was joined by William Smith, a medical graduate from

Edinburgh University, and together they established the American School of Osteopathy.

During the twentieth century the number of trained osteopathic practitioners in America has grown. It has gained legal and professional status and by 1973 full rights to practice were granted in all states of America. In 1917 Martin Littlejohn established the first osteopathy school in London. Osteopathic practice in the United Kingdom and Europe is less well accepted than in the United States and practice is limited to straightforward manipulation.

Theory and principles

Still stressed the importance of clear neural and vascular pathways which would maintain the body as a balanced, working unit. He emphasised the understanding of the exact structure and function of the human musculoskeletal mechanism in order to establish normal equilibrium in form and function. In its normal mechanical state the body can mount its own defences, and repair itself, against pathologic conditions. Disease may result when this balance or equilibrium is affected then disease may result. Movement and circulation of body fluids are important to maintaining health. The nerves control fluids and their movement.

Application and practice
Examination of the patient
The patient is observed sitting, standing, lying and moving from side to side. The osteopath notes the range of joint function and feels muscles, ligaments, and soft tissues. Reflexes should also be tested, and X-rays can be used to check the extent of any internal damage or problem. Clinical laboratory tests may also be used to identify further disease states in order to reach a full diagnosis.

Any predisposing factors such as habitual or occupational posture, vertebral problems, muscle tension from stress, infection, joint damage or other physical problems are assessed. Any of these conditions can affect the vertebrae. Interference with the mechanical function of any particular vertebrae or spinal segment reflects some dysfunction elsewhere in the body.

Emotional, as well as physical, tension, infections, over-exercise or immobility can contribute to irritation, pain and muscle tension. This tension can result in lack of blood to the muscles and tissues, swelling and inflammation which can cause a problem with movement and function as well as result in fibrous scarring.

Treatment focuses on correcting the problem using a combination of medication, surgery, physiotherapy and education in diet and lifestyle. This means that the whole patient, rather than the simple disease, is treated. Osteopathy is particularly valuable in treating whiplash injuries, scoliosis or curvature of the spine, other spinal problems including thoracic, or chest, problems and sacroiliac or low back pain, dysmenorrhea or painful periods, and cardiac or pulmonary conditions.

Treatment
Osteopathy is applicable to all disease states. Treatment is based on evaluating the whole body as a whole unit rather than examining and treating one organ system at a time. It is based on patient's signs and symptoms, individual history and examination of the musculoskeletal system. Any local asymmetry, restriction of movement and changes indicating postural tension are treated in order to relieve neural and vascular blockages which cause the symptoms.

Manipulation is considered to be a central part of osteopathic therapy. It ranges from manual reduction of fractures, dislocations and joint

Osteopathy

problems to externally applied cardiac massage and postural drainage for pulmonary diseases.

If the condition can be treated then the osteopath will advise the patient on posture, relaxation and exercises. The osteopath will then manipulate the area to encourage relaxation of the joint and increase its movement. Manipulation is based on the principle of moving muscles against a direct counterforce. These are known as muscle energy techniques and are classified as isotonic (concentric) or isometric contractions. This encourages movement in stiff joints by strengthening weak muscles, stretching muscles and improving circulation. The range of movement is carried out against increased tension or resistance. It is important that the specific force used, and the particular muscle group being exercised, are carefully monitored and controlled in order to achieve success.

Massage may also be used along with manipulation, again to encourage blood flow. If the condition is a long-standing one then the patient may experience some temporary increased discomfort but this should resolve quickly.

Other techniques include myofascial, counterstrain and thrusting techniques. Myofascial treatment results in relaxation of contracted, or tense, muscles, increased circulation, and increased vascular and lymphatic drainage. There is also some interest in the use of trigger points to achieve the same results.

Counterstrain techniques are based on the principle that mechanical dysfunction has a neuromuscular basis. Diagnosis is made finding reflex tender points either above or below, or in front or behind, the affected vertebral segment. The treatment is positional and relieves pain by passive pulling of the joint and by reducing and stopping the inappropriate movement.

Thrusting techniques involve moving the dysfunctional joint through its restricted range of movement.

T'AI CHI

T'ai chi is a Chinese martial art form which stresses graceful and fluid movement in order to assist the development of the qi – the internal spirit.

It is useful for muscle tension, back pain, poor posture, loss of stamina and hypertension. It is also helpful for those suffering from stress, tension and poor self-esteem.

T'ai chi is a gentle and relaxed martial art and it can be practised by elderly people quit safely. It does not require any particular strength or level of fitness, and people of any age can start studying t'ai chi. It does need stamina and balance and if there are any doubts then advice should be sought from your GP.

Although t'ai chi can be studied and learnt from video and books it is best learnt from a trained teacher who can demonstrate the combination of movements in person. Comfortable, loose clothing is all the equipment that is required.

History and origins

T'ai chi was practised as early as 1122 BC during the Chou dynasty in China. A form of exercise call daoyin was popular which combined breathing and body movements. Lao-tzu, who founded Taoism, identified the philosophy that qi – the life force – could be controlled by the mind. During the later Han dynasty Buddhists travelled to China from India bringing the principles and practice of yoga. Some of the basic yoga ideas, as well as the sport of boxing, were combined with the practice of daoyin. This eventually became qigong and later t'ai chi. A Taoist boxer, Chang San-feng, developed a new series of exercises based on Taoist philosophy. He believed that the body should be flexible and strong, and that movements should flow naturally and gracefully. Thus body movements, the belief in the ability to manipulate the qi and the breathing of qigong evolved into t'ai chi. It was initially a form of self-defence but later it became a system of physical training, spiritual development and lifestyle.

Theory and principles

T'ai chi teachers emphasise that it is not just a

system of external physical movement but an internal art as well. There are three basic treasures – the ching, the ch'i (qi) and the shen. The exercises concentrate on the development of inner calm in order that the mind can regulate the body. The movements are all slow, graceful and natural. Each movement flows naturally into another. The body should be held in a semi-crouched position in order to maximise balance. It is also important to keep a steady breathing rhythm.

Many of the routines have interesting names which conjure vivid pictures and help remember the order of the movements. It is ideal for older people and those who are less physically strong or athletic.

THERMAL (HEAT) AND CRYO (COLD) THERAPIES

Heat therapy is the application of heat to the body for healing. Cryotherapy is the application of ice, water or freezer packs to assist therapy. The two are often used together.

Heat therapy is used for cramps, muscle injuries or pain, indigestion, arthritic pain, stomach ache, colds and wounds.

Cold therapy can be used for fevers, burns, sprains and bruises, swelling and inflammation, arthritic pain and other joint pain, athletic injuries, headaches, skin problems, bites, stings and boils, itching and heat exhaustion.

Pregnant women, the elderly, very young children, those with heart conditions, high blood pressure or other circulation problems, including those associated with diabetes, should not be subject to extremes of temperature.

The equipment is quite simple. Either cold water, ice packs, freezer packs, hot water bottles, heating pads, hot cloths, heat lamps, sauna, steam room and hot water.

Origins and history

Greeks, Romans and Egyptians used heat for therapeutic purposes and it is known that Chinese and Ayurvedic medicine used heat as part of their healing procedures. In China heat was sometimes used with acupuncture to stimulate a point. The leaf of the wormwood tree – the moxa – would be lit and placed on the body at an acupuncture point. This process is known as moxibustion. The Romans were very proud of their bath houses where there were hot and cold baths, massages and plunge pools. Native Americans used sweat lodges – highly heated rooms – to assist healing. Herbs were often used in part of the heat treatment.

Cold therapy or cold baths were recommended by Hippocrates in the fifth century BC. The Romans used cold plunges as part of their bathing process. They would jump from a very cold pool into a hot one and then repeat the process. The stimulation achieved was very like that obtained during the Scandinavian tradition of saunas. After treatment in a Native American sweat house the sufferer would be taken outside and dipped in a cold stream.

Thermal and cryo therapies

Application and practice

Heat therapy is cheap and easy and has widespread application. It is often best combined with cold therapy. Heat increases the heart rate, dilates the blood vessels and increases circulation. Heat is not a good treatment for those who are suffering from any inflammation. A good rule of thumb is, if the affected part of the body is already hot then cold therapy is more beneficial. Heat is useful for aches and pains, arthritis, colds and flu and stress.

Heat can be applied to the whole body in the form of a bath or sauna but it can also be applied to a specific part as required either by massage or by applying a local source of heat.

Cold therapy is useful for injuries and sprains. Cold constricts the blood flow and has some numbing effect which is useful as a short-term local anaesthetic. Cold therapy is particularly useful for burns, sprains, nosebleeds, headaches, stings, sunburn, swelling and bruises. Cold can be applied by immersion in a cold bath, although it should be ensured that the bath is not too cold. It is often best to start with a tepid bath and then cool it gradually.

Contrast therapy – where heat and cold is used alternately – is often very useful. Dilating then contracting of the blood vessels increases the pumping action which circulates blood round the body. This increased circulation improves the flow of oxygen as well as remove waste and toxins more rapidly.

Contrasting hot and cold baths can help muscle and joint pain, as well as general stiffness and aches. The affected area can be soaked in a hot (approximately 104°) bath for five minutes then immersed in cold (approximately 59°) water for a couple of minutes. This alternating immersion can be repeated for about twenty minutes.

A similar treatment may be useful for migraine headaches. Some people experience relief from their symptoms by alternating hot and cold showers.

YOGA

Yoga uses systems of movement, breathing and meditation which are designed to unify and balance the mind and body. There are different systems of yoga, some consist of breathing exercises and postures and others involve contemplation meditation. At the same time it can also used as a form of physical exercise.

Yoga is useful for muscle tension, backache, headaches, poor circulation, posture, obesity, constipation, asthma and other bronchial problems, menstrual problems, peptic ulcers, diabetes, sinus congestions, stress, insomnia, anxiety, tension and fatigue. There are no contraindications to yoga.

History and origins
Yoga derives from the ancient Hindu tradition of India. Ayurveda, the science of the body, is studied first before studying yoga. The spiritual aspect of yoga can only be practised once the body is fit. It

originated 5000 years ago although it may be even older. Yoga, in Sanskrit, is yuj, which translates as union. This emphasises the importance of total spiritual and physical union.

Only a few philosophers and theologians followed the principles of yoga. They taught their followers the knowledge and skills to practise the system. The first principles were identified by Patanjali who lived about 300 BC. He described the eight limbs of yoga and yogic practices. These are: natural regulation of the nervous system, discipline, cleansing, postures, concentration, contemplation, awareness and the state of perfect equilibrium.

Theory and principles
Although there are different systems of yoga they all have the same purpose of unity of the mind and body. The different yoga systems include: raja, jnana, karma, bakti and hatha. The hatha system is the one which is taught in the west. It involves exercises and positions. The other systems involve more mental control and concentration, particularly the raja yoga which is the yoga of meditation.

Hatha yoga includes postures which are called asanas and breathing – pranayama. It is believed that the body's essence is contained in the pran or breath. If the breathing is changed then general health can be improved. Controlling the breathing, particularly during a period of emotional distress, can help a feeling of calm and peace.

The postures or asanas are easy to learn and practising them can increase flexibility and control. It is important never to force or strain a position or movement. Although some postures look impossible to perform at the beginning with practice they will become easier. A yoga teacher should stress the importance of patience to help movement and position. Each different position should be held for one or two minutes, and the ultimate aim is to produce a feeling of relaxation and tranquillity.

Application and practice
It is best to attend a class for proper instruction and to carry out exercises before mealtimes. Comfortable clothes are important and a folded blanket or rug should be used to provide a base. There are some basic positions which are useful for a beginner.

The first one is the 'spinal twist' which is done sitting on the floor with the legs outstretched. The left leg should be bent and put over the right leg. After exhalation the body should then be twisted to the left, and the right hand moved towards the right foot. The body should be supported by the left hand on the ground and the back should be kept straight. With each exhalation the body should be twisted further to the left, and the position held for about a minute. The whole movement should then be repeated this time turning to the right.

The 'half-shoulder stand' starts lying on the back with the legs raised. During exhalation the hips are lifted and the legs moved so that they pass over the head. The weight of the body should be on the shoulders, elbows and arms. The position should be held for several minutes and respiration should be normal. Return the arms to the floor and the body is then gradually returned to the lying positions during inhalation.

The 'bridge' starts from a lying position. The knees should be bent, the legs separated and the arms placed at the side of the body. During inhalation the body and legs should be lifted to form a bridge position. Link the fingers under the body and rotate the body from side to side, keeping the shoulders in the same position. The bridge posture should be held for at least a minute after inhalation before returning to a normal lying position.

The 'bow' involves lying on the ground and the knees bent and raised towards the head. The hand should hold the ankles and, during inhalation, the ankles should be pulled so that the chest, head and tights are raised off the floor. The final position should be held for about ten breaths and then, after the final exhalation, the legs should be released.

The 'triangle' starts in an upright position, legs apart and arms held out at shoulder level. The right foot should be extended and, during exhalation, bend down towards the right, moving the right hand down the leg towards the ankle. The body should not move forward and, as the body bends, the left arm should be lifted up with the palm facing to the front. This posture should be held for a minute, during which time the stretch should be extended as far as is comfortable. After inhalation the routine should be repeated in the opposite direction.

Another useful exercise is known as the 'corpse'. Lie on the back, legs outstretched, heels slightly apart and legs flopping outwards. The arms should rest on the floor, palms up and fingers slightly curled. Breathing should be through the nostrils not the mouth. Take two deep breaths and exhale fully each time. Allow the abdominal muscles to relax and return to normal. Breathing should become smooth and rhythmic. Focus on each part of the body and release any tension until the whole body is relaxed.

Another, quite complex, routine, known as 'a greeting to the sun', involves twelve different positions. Stand upright and hold the palms of the hands next to the chest. Inhale and stretch the arms upright, with the palms turning towards the ceiling and gradually lean backwards. Exhale and, with the legs straight, the hands should be placed onto the ground. With a deep inhalation bend the knees, then place one leg out backwards, with the knee touching the ground. With both hands on the ground the head should be raised and the hips pushed forwards. Next, both legs should be stretched out backwards together as the breath is held. The body should be raised off the ground. After exhaling the body should be folded over, knees bent, so that the head touches the ground with the arms stretched out in front. After a deep breath in and out, the body should be positioned face down and supported by the hands and toes – the stomach and hips should not touch the ground. The hips should then be raised so the body is an inverted V-shape. Return to kneeling position with the head touching the ground. After inhaling one leg should be stretched out behind, as carried out at the beginning of the exercise – although this time it should be the opposite leg which is stretched. Finally, the feet should be placed together and the legs straightened. Bend down towards the floor and place the hands on the floor on either side of the feet. Inhale and then stand up straight. This procedure can be carried out several times if desired.

OTHER HEALING THERAPIES

There are a number of other therapies or behaviours which can help achieve a state of emotional and physical well being. These can include special diets and special therapies such as dream therapy, visualisation, affirmation or biofeedback. There are other occupations or behaviours which can also have a therapeutic effect such as art, music, gardening or pet therapy. This latter group may seem no more than hobbies but they are all activities which relax, distract and stimulate. They are only helpful if they are pleasurable and not a task. Some of these can be done individually or they can be carried out as part of a group activity or class. Local schools often offer adult evening classes for those who want to learn some basic techniques. There are also some specialists who are trained professional therapists who use art, music or drama as a form of counselling. However, it is not always necessary to attend a therapist to enjoy the benefits of these relaxing activities.

Art therapy

Art therapy can help headaches, stroke victims, those with arthritis and rheumatism, drug and alcohol dependency, emotional problems and stress.

It is not necessary to have any particular talent but it is a process of finding out what is most enjoyable, relaxing and rewarding. It may be modelling, oil painting, charcoal sketching or water colours. All or one of these may prove suitable. Art may be a medium through which to express non-verbal thoughts and emotions, which in turn help release stress or tension, but at the same time it can also be seen less analytically than this. It can also be a hobby which is enjoyable and therefore it will be doing some good.

Other healing therapies

Music therapy

Music, whether as an active participant in playing an instrument or simply listening to it, can also have therapeutic value in the same way as art.

It can help asthmatics, those with high blood pressure, headaches, pain, trauma, stroke victims, dementia and other physical disabilities. It is also useful for sleep disorders, anxiety, depression, stress and learning disabilities.

Again music therapy can be self- administered or offered as part of a professional therapy programme. The form, tempo and style of the music chosen is important as it can either slow down bodily functions in a relaxing, soothing manner or stimulate and energise with an up-tempo rhythm. Faster, louder music can be used for fast exercise routines or other physical activities. A quiet, calm rhythm can help relaxation, perhaps as part of a meditation or slow exercise routine. Also a loud and energetic tune may help to release anger and other emotions, and restore a more balanced emotional state. A sad ballad or tune may release feelings of sadness which can be cathartic. Similarly an uplifting and cheerful piece can increase positive, happy feelings.

Garden therapy and others

Gardening, caring for a pet or participating in drama workshops or clubs can also have therapeutic benefits which do not need to be professionally organised or managed. Professional therapy in these forms is available, and for those who are quite clearly physically or psychologically unwell they may be offered as part of their treatment programme. For the rest self-motivated participation in any of the above can increase the quality of life and well being.